SAMPSON TECHNICAL COLLEGE

THE CHRISTIAN YEAR

ITS PURPOSE AND ITS HISTORY

THE CHRISTIAN YEAR

ITS PURPOSE AND ITS HISTORY

BY THE
REV. WALKER GWYNNE, D.D.

NEW IMPRESSION

LONGMANS, GREEN, AND CO.
FOURTH AVENUE & 30TH STREET, NEW YORK
LONDON, BOMBAY, CALCUTTA AND MADRAS
1917

Republished by Grand River Books, Detroit, 1971

Library of Congress Catalog Card Number 74-89269

INTRODUCTION

THE lack and the need of a popular manual on the Christian Year were forced on the attention of the writer when he undertook to teach a class in the Newark Diocesan Training School for Teachers. His aim in the present volume is to provide such a book as an intelligent teacher would desire, giving, not merely the bare facts concerning the different festivals and fasts, but also some account of the practical and devotional reasons which the whole Catholic Church has had from the beginning for adopting the system of her Christian Year and Calendar.

So far as defence or *apologia* is concerned, Hooker with his lofty philosophical treatment of the subject is of course unexcelled. But Hooker is not accessible to the average student, and his somewhat antiquated style, in spite of its nobility and charm, is not likely to attract the ordinary reader of to-day. There are only a few monographs in English on the Christian Year, intended chiefly for candidates for Holy Orders, of which the latest and most useful are " The Church Year and the Calendar " by the late Bishop Dowden of Edinburgh, and " The Liturgical Year " by the Rev. Vernon Staley. Of the latter there is an abridgment entitled " The Seasons, etc., of the Christian Year." " Heortology, a History of the Christian Festivals from their Origin to the present Day," by Professor Kellner of the University of Bonn,[1] is probably the most complete monograph on the subject, but its treatment is almost wholly technical and historical. As its author is a Roman Catholic it occasionally shows, as might be expected, some marked leanings. For the rest, the writer was compelled to search in encyclopædias, and books on liturgics, most of which, however, contain only dry-as-dust information as to dates and authorities and origins, which are chiefly of interest to the liturgical student or archæologist. In this respect, however, he would single out as of especial value Chapter VIII of "Origines du Culte Chrétien," by Duchesne, of which an English translation by M. L. McClure is published by the S.P.C.K. (London, 1903); the 20th and 21st books of Bingham's "Antiquities of the Christian Church," and chapters 6, 7, and 8, in "The Ministry of Grace" by Bishop John Wordsworth of Salisbury.

It may be well to mention here for the ordinary reader that the original sources of information on the Church Year are to be found in early Church historians, missals, and other service books, decrees of Church councils, official documents, sermons preached on festival days, early calendars, and hymnaries.

For much that the author has written on the Calendar he is indebted to an excellent volume on "The Theory and Use of the Church Calendar in the Measurement of Time," by his former preceptor, the late Professor Samuel Seabury, D.D., of the General Theological Seminary, New York, a grandson of the first American Bishop.

Of the many devotional books on the Christian Year probably the best and most useful modern volume is that of the late Arthur Cleveland Coxe, Bishop of Western

[1] English translation, 1908, Kegan Paul & Co.

INTRODUCTION

New York, entitled "Thoughts on the Services," a new issue of which, edited by Bishop Whitehead of Pittsburgh, is published by the Lippincott Co. of Philadelphia. Of poetry it is needless to say that Keble's "Christian Year" and "Lyra Innocentium," and Mrs. Alexander's "Hymns for Little Children," take the lead in charm and devotional feeling. Bishop Ken's "Hymns for All Festivals of the Christian Year,"[1] amid much that is dull, contains a few poems of real worth. In George Herbert, Spenser, Wordsworth, Tennyson, and the "Lyra Apostolica" (containing poems by Newman, Keble, and others), the "Lyra Messianica" by Orby Shipley, "Lyra Catholica" by E. Caswall, "Lyra Sanctorum" (for the Minor Festivals), "The Cathedral" by Isaac Williams, and Palgrave's "Treasury of Sacred Song," besides the Hymnals, much illustrative poetry may also be found.

While the author makes no pretensions to original liturgical lore, he believes that his treatment of the various subjects has the support of the latest and best scholarship. He hopes, moreover, that the little book may be found useful, not only in his own communion, but also in other bodies of English-speaking Christians, whose growing tendency is to return to the ancient and well-tried methods of the historic Church in matters of worship and festival. It has been wisely said that, "By the changes of day and night, of seasons and years, Creation calls upon man to raise his mind to God at stated times, and to enter into communion with Him."[2] It may be that the observance together of the great immemorial days and seasons of the Christian Year which, through all the centuries, have made Christians

---

[1] 1721; new ed. by Pickering, 1868.
[2] Kellner's *Heortology*, p. 1.

to kneel together before their common Lord, in a common worship, will prove the most effective method, above mere argument, for bringing about that visible unity for which, with dying breath, the Lord Jesus pleaded with the One God and Father of us all.

CONTENTS

INTRODUCTION

PAGE

The Need of a Popular Manual—Hooker's defence of the Christian Year—Bishop Dowden—Vernon Staley—Professor Kellner—Duchesne—Professor Seabury—Original Sources—Devotional and Poetical Aspects.............. v

CHAPTER I

WHY THE CHURCH HAS A CHRISTIAN YEAR

The System "broad-based" on Human Reason and Experience—Pagan Religions, Modern Christian Bodies, and Civil Governments all Alike in their Use of Anniversaries and Commemorations—Bishop Arthur Cleveland Coxe on the Value of the Christian Year—Hooker's Judgment........ 1

CHAPTER II

PURITAN OBJECTIONS

Hooker's Philosophic Defence of the Church's System—Action of the Puritan Parliament in 1644—Abuse of Good Customs no Reason for their Destruction—Even the Sabbath Perverted and Abused by Ancient Jews, as Sunday is by Modern Christians.................................... 7

CHAPTER III

THE CHURCH YEAR A GROWTH

Its "Root" in the Divinely Appointed Ritual Year of the Church of Israel—Its "Branch" in the Incarnate Life of

Christ—A Full Account not to be expected in the New Testament—Continuity and Fulfilment of the Church of Israel in the Church of Christ.......................... 11

CHAPTER IV

THE RITUAL YEAR OF THE CHURCH OF ISRAEL

The Sabbath not Jewish, but Universal—The other Sacred Festivals Historical—Passover, Pentecost, Tabernacles, Feast of Trumpets, or New Year, Purim, Dedication, or Feast of Lights, Great Day of Atonement—Names of the Jewish Months—Dr. Edersheim on the Effect of the Ritual Year on the Imagination of Jewish Children............. 15

CHAPTER V

THE JEWISH YEAR AND THE APOSTOLIC CHURCH

Under this System Christ and His Apostles were Trained from Childhood—To these Laws and Customs our Lord was Supremely Loyal—He Chooses Two of the Great Feasts of Israel with which to associate His Death and Resurrection, the Coming of the Holy Ghost and the Establishment of His Church.......................... 22

CHAPTER VI

THE BEGINNINGS OF THE CHRISTIAN YEAR IN THE APOSTOLIC CHURCH

The First Christians were all Jews who faithfully observed the Ancient Festivals and Fasts, but saw in them the "Body" where formerly there was but a "Shadow of Good Things to Come"—Passover and Pentecost—"The First Day of the Week," being the Day of the Resurrection, observed in Addition to the Sabbath as a "Sister Day"... 28

CHAPTER VII

THE VALUE OF CUSTOM AND TRADITION IN THE CHURCH

S. Paul's Valuation of Customs and Traditions—The Worth of Customs and Traditions to a Nation and to Individuals—

CONTENTS

All Traditions not of Equal Obligation—The Test "from the Beginning"—"Sursum Corda"—The Holy Scriptures and the Sacred Ministry Supreme Examples of Tradition—What then is the Purpose of Holy Scripture?—Archbishop Alexander, Scott Holland, Dean Hook, Dr. E. Hawkins... 35

CHAPTER VIII

THE CHURCH CALENDAR AND ITS USE

Greek and Roman Calendars—*Anno Domini*, or the Year of Our Lord—Why not adopted till the Year 541—Dionysius Exiguus—What we owe to Julius Cæsar—Error of the Calendar in A. D. 1582—"New Style" adopted by Churches in Communion with Rome—Not adopted by England till 1752—Greek and Russian Churches retain the "Old Style." 43

CHAPTER IX

TECHNICAL WORDS IN THE CALENDAR

Lunar Cycle, Metonic Cycle, Golden Number, or Prime, Paschal Moon, Epact, Dominical Letter, Bissextile or Leap Year, Ferial and Festal, Vigil and Eve, Octave, Movable and Immovable Feasts 47

CHAPTER X

THE BEGINNING OF THE CHURCH YEAR—ADVENT AND CHRISTMAS

Great Variety in Details of Calendars, but One Central Principle, the Incarnation—The Purpose of Advent—Other Names for Christmas—The Meaning and History of "Mass"—Why December 25? 53

CHAPTER XI

OTHER IMMOVABLE FEASTS OF OUR LORD

Circumcision, Epiphany, Presentation in the Temple, Annunciation, Transfiguration.............................. 58

CONTENTS

CHAPTER XII

THE MOVABLE FEASTS—EASTER AND ASCENSION

Why Easter not Immovable like Christmas—(For Origin of Easter see Chapters IV and V; for Origin of Sunday see Chapter VI.) Great Importance attached to Easter seen in the Quartodeciman Controversy—How finally settled in the Church at the Council of Nice, A.D. 325—Why the British and Irish Rule for Easter differed from that of Italy—Ascension Day—"The Pilgrimage of Silvia".... 64

CHAPTER XIII

OTHER MOVABLE FEASTS—WHITSUNDAY AND TRINITY

The Coming of the Holy Ghost and the Birthday of the Church—The Name Whitsunday—The calling of Sundays "after Trinity" instead of "after Pentecost, or Whitsunday," peculiar to the English Church, and to the German Churches founded by the English 70

CHAPTER XIV

THE SAINTS' DAYS

Hooker on their Observance—Red-letter and Black-letter Days—The Special Value of Black-letter Days—Why a Saint's Day is called *Dies natalis*, or Birthday—Appropriateness of the Time of the Nativities of the Baptist and of Our Lord—Also the Days given to S. Andrew, S. Thomas, S. Stephen, S. John the Evangelist, and the Holy Innocents—The Origin of Saints' Days—Bishop Westcott, Bishop Ellicott, and Dr. Newman on Saints' Days........ 75

CHAPTER XV

THE FEAST OF S. MICHAEL AND ALL ANGELS

Only Two Angels mentioned by Name in the Canonical Scriptures—Two also in "the Books Called Apocrypha"—The Prominence given by Our Lord and the Holy Scriptures to Angels—The Great Practical Purpose of the Revelation of the Ministry of Angels—Hooker on the Angels.... 82

CONTENTS

CHAPTER XVI

THE FEAST OF ALL SAINTS

All Hallows and Hallowe'en—The Great Need of such a Day of Remembrance—Paradise not Heaven—The Intermediate State only a Place of Preparation for Heaven—The American Day of National Thanksgiving...................... 87

CHAPTER XVII

THE BLACK-LETTER DAYS

The Revision of the Old English Calendar in 1661 imperfect—The Present English Calendar, with Notes on the Black-letter Days... 92

CHAPTER XVIII

THE FASTS OF THE CHRISTIAN YEAR

Fasts equally with Festivals open to Abuse—Yet the New Testament as well as the Old full of Accounts of Fasting—The Example of Christ and His Apostles—The True Purpose of Fasting—The English-speaking Church lays down no Hard and Narrow Rules for Fasting............ 101

CHAPTER XIX

LENT AND PRE-LENT

The Words Lent and Quadragesima—Meaning of the Names of the Pre-Lenten Sundays—Early Origin of the Fast in Preparation for Easter—Blunt on the Original Object of Lent—Ash-Wednesday and Shrove-Tuesday—Mid-Lent, or Refreshment Sunday.............................. 106

CHAPTER XX

HOLY WEEK

Not "Passion Week"—The Events of Palm Sunday, and the four following Days—Maundy Thursday, why so called 110

CONTENTS

CHAPTER XXI

GOOD FRIDAY AND EASTER EVEN

PAGE

Good Friday kept at first as a Feast Day in connection with Easter—After the Decision of the Church to observe Easter always on a Sunday, Good Friday naturally acquired its Present Character—Consecration of the Eucharist, but not Reception, began early to be omitted on Good Friday—Called the "Mass of the Pre-Sanctified"—Blunt on the Disuse of this Custom in the Church of England—The practice of Bishop King of Lincoln, Dean Church, Dean Gregory, and Dr. Liddon—Easter Even.... 114

CHAPTER XXII

OTHER DAYS OF FASTING

Ember and Rogation Days—Fridays—Vigils and Eves.... 120

CHAPTER XXIII

VARIATIONS AND REVISIONS OF CALENDARS

The Use of Liturgies Universal in the Primitive Church—Leading Features Common to All, yet Many Variations in Detail—Meaning of the Word "Use"—Various Revisions of the Liturgies of Rome and England—Need of Revision also in the Calendars, especially of Black-letter Days—Some Peculiarities of the Roman and Oriental Calendars.. 124

APPENDIX

THE LITURGICAL COLORS................................. 131
LEADING QUESTIONS FOR REVIEW OR EXAMINATION.......... 133
INDEX... 137

THE CHRISTIAN YEAR
ITS PURPOSE AND ITS HISTORY

CHAPTER I

WHY THE CHURCH HAS A CHRISTIAN YEAR

"The way before us lies
Distinct with signs, through which in set career,
As through a zodiac, moves the ritual year."
—*Wordsworth,* "*Eccles. Sonnets,*" XIX.

"Our festival year is a bulwark of orthodoxy as real as our confessions of faith."—*Archer Butler.*

THE question of the age or origin of particular festivals or fasts is not so important as the practical and historical grounds on which the Christian Year is founded. No apology in the modern sense of the word is needed for its use, but rather an *apologia* or *rationale* to show how the system is "broad based" on reason and human experience as well as on the divine will. It has been well said indeed that "The foundations and heart of the whole festal system of the Church were given by a Higher Hand, and only the development—the much less important part of the whole—is to be attributed to the thoughts of men."[1]

The Christian Year may then be described (1) as a

[1] Kellner's *Heortology*, p. 203.

scheme which provides a dramatic method of commemorating, at special seasons and on special days, the chief events of the Incarnate Life of our Lord. (2) It provides for the worshipper a well-rounded system of Scripture lessons, epistles and gospels, and selected psalms and hymns, for the purpose of securing what S. Paul calls "the proportion (*analogia*) of the faith",[1] that is, a symmetrical framework invaluable to preacher and people alike, saving them from the evils of sensationalism and distorted teaching, and from the exaggeration or over-emphasis of one set of truths at the expense of others equally important. (3) It recalls the main features of some noble lives recorded in the New Testament besides that of our Lord; also the lives of notable men and women in the Church's history after these first days; showing how Christlike were many of His servants all through the centuries. It thus testifies also to the historic continuity of the Church from the Apostles' days, while proclaiming the fact that real sainthood or imitation of Christ is not an impossibility, but is within the reach of all. Moreover (4), true to the experience of our daily life, it provides for variety of devotional tone in alternate fast and festival, which it makes manifest also to the eye by means of ecclesiastical colors adapted to the seasons.

The Christian Year is thus the skeleton on which the Prayer Book and the whole system of the Church's teaching are framed. It is true a skeleton in itself is not a thing of delight, yet nevertheless there can be neither life nor beauty without it in flower, or tree, or man. It is the necessary framework on which to lay the flesh and blood and color of the living man or the living plant.

[1] Rom. xii. 6.

It is important therefore at the outset to understand that in the observance of a ritual year there is nothing forced or artificial. Such a plan is strictly in accordance with human nature as testified to by all history, pagan, Jewish, and Christian alike. Egyptians and Assyrians, Greeks and Romans, all had their festivals and fasts. The people of Israel had a ritual year by divine direction and particular ordinances. Nor are such observances confined to religious systems. Even civil governments, modern as well as ancient, have always found it necessary to have their national anniversaries and commemorations. When the revolutionary and infidel government of France rejected the ancient ritual year of the Church, and even the old civil year which took its date from the birth of Christ (*Anno Domini*), it was forced to coin new names for the months, to each of which it gave thirty days uniformly, and it ordained a system of five festival days wherewith to fill out the year, placing them from September 17th to 21st. These it devoted respectively to "The Virtues, Genius, Labor, Opinion, and Rewards." Moreover, instead of the weekly Sunday it made only one day in ten a holiday. But human nature at length rebelled, and the scheme lasted less than fourteen years, namely, from Sept. 22, 1792, the date of the establishment of the Republic, till Jan. 1, 1806. So likewise, without formally rejecting the Christian Year, America has its Fourth of July or Independence Day, its Washington's and Lincoln's birthdays, its Columbus Day, its Thanksgiving, Decoration, Labor, and Arbor Days.

Even those religious bodies whose forefathers rejected the Christian Year, have their " Flower Sunday," their " Hospital," " Children's," " Peace," and " Temperance " Sundays, their " Rally Day," and " Week of Prayer," and are ever coining other special days of observance. Moreover, along with this, most happily, they are almost universally adopting much which they once rejected. Easter Day is now observed by nearly all of them. They are beginning to keep Holy Week, if not Lent, and they observe Christmas socially, if not yet on its religious side. All which goes to show how deeply rooted in human nature and in human need is this principle of associating great truths with times and seasons. It is the principle in fact laid down by God in the Fourth Commandment of the moral law, where the Sabbath is made the commemoration of God's rest from the work of creation, and the pledge of that future " Sabbath rest " which " remaineth for the people of God." [1]

Bishop Coxe is writing concerning the Christian Year when he says: " Look at this majestic system of claiming all time for Christ, and filling every day in every year with His Name, and His Worship. See how vast and rich the scheme, as a token of, and a provision for, the Second Advent. . . . God is the real author of this scheme, and it is revealed, in its substance, as part of His Wisdom for perpetuating His Truth. . . . And yet because all this is but part of our inestimable inheritance as Churchmen, we hardly think of it as, even on popular grounds, a conclusive reason for being what we are, and as furnishing an irresistible argument against those who oppose themselves. Of course we are Churchmen on higher grounds, and for independent reasons: yet it is a fact that the mind of our countrymen is too much perverted and prejudiced to appreciate these higher principles. We can hardly refer to them without wounding their feelings, and exciting their antagonism. But might we not safely and charitably direct their attention to our Liturgic System, first of all, as something

[1] Heb. iv. 9; Rev. Ver.

which they ought to examine; and then leave them to their own conclusions, when once they shall have discovered that this inestimable possession is only to be found in its completeness among those who have preserved all the other Apostolic institutions of the Gospel in their purity and integrity?"[1]

"The Judicious" Hooker, as he was well named, the contemporary of Shakespeare and Bacon, with his keen philosophic mind and balanced judgment, sets the question of a ritual year on the highest plane of practical wisdom and necessity. It is not a question of personal preference or æsthetics. It is a matter which has the stamp and approval, not only of nature in its best estate, but of the Holy Scriptures, and the Church in all the ages. "All things whatsoever having their time," he writes, "the works of God have always that time which is seasonable and fittest for them. His works are some ordinary, some more rare, all worthy of observation, but not of all like necessity to be remembered; they all have their times, but they do not add the same estimation and glory to the times wherein they are. For as God by being everywhere yet doth not give unto all *places* one and the same degree of holiness, so neither [does He give] one and the same dignity to all *times* by working in all. For if all, either places or times, were in respect of God alike, wherefore was it said unto Moses by particular designation, 'This very place wherein thou standest is holy ground'?[2] Why doth the Prophet David choose out of all the days of the year but one whereof he speaketh by way of principal admiration, 'This is the day which the Lord hath made'?[3] No doubt, as God's extraordinary presence hath hallowed

[1] *Thoughts on the Services*, pp. 17, 18.
[2] Ex. iii. 5. [3] Psalm cxviii. 24.

and sanctified certain *places,* so they are His extraordinary works that have truly and worthily advanced certain *times,* for which cause they ought to be, with all men that honour God, more holy than other days." [1]

He then quotes from that uncanonical but wonderfully wise book, "Ecclesiasticus, or the Wisdom of Sirach, the Son of Jesus," [2] "Why doth one day excel another, when as all the light of every day in the year is of the sun? By the knowledge of the Lord they were distinguished; and He altered seasons and feasts. Some of them hath He made high days, and hallowed them, and some of them hath He made ordinary days."

Hooker sums up his account of the festal system of the Church in these eloquent words: " Well to celebrate these religious and sacred days is to spend the flower of our time happily. They are the splendor and outward dignity of our religion, forcible witnesses of ancient truth, provocations to the exercise of all piety, shadows of our endless felicity in heaven, on earth everlasting records and memorials, wherein they who cannot be drawn to hearken to what we teach, may, only by looking on what we do, in a manner read whatsoever we believe." [3]

[1] *Ecc. Polity*, V. lxx., pp. 489, 490, Keble's ed.
[2] xxxiii. 7, 8, 9.
[3] *Ecc. Polity*, V. lxxii, pp. 518, 519, Keble's ed.

CHAPTER II

PURITAN OBJECTIONS

"If these beautiful arts—architecture, painting, music, and the like—detain men on their own account, to wonder at their own intrinsic charms, down among the things of sense,—if we are thinking more of music than of Him whose glory it heralds, more of the beauty of form and color than of Him whose temple it adorns,—then, be sure, we are robbing God of His glory; we are turning His temple into a den of thieves. No error is without its element of truth, and jealousy on this point was the strength of Puritanism, which made it a power notwithstanding its violence,—notwithstanding its falsehood."—*H. P. Liddon*, Sermon on *Intruders in the Temple.*

IN spite of the natural fitness of the Christian Year to men's spiritual needs, as we have remarked in the preceding chapter, the Church of England met with great and bitter opposition in regard to its observance from the Puritans in the sixteenth and seventeenth centuries. Hooker, in his splendid defence of the Church against these narrow views, speaks of " the difference in days " as being " natural and necessary." " Even nature," he says, " hath taught the heathens, and God the Jews, and Christ us, that festival solemnities are a part of the public exercise of religion." [1] He quotes S. Augustine as saying, " By festival solemnities and set days we dedicate and sanctify to God the memory of His benefits, lest unthankful forgetfulness thereof should creep upon us in course of time." [2] And Hooker further adds: " The very law of nature itself, which all

[1] *Ecc. Pol.*, V. lxx., pp. 490–494.   [2] Pp. 495, 6.

men confess to be God's law, requireth in government no less the sanctification of times, than of places, persons, and things, unto God's honor." [1] It was God who said to Moses at the Bush, "The place whereon thou standest is holy ground," and it was God also who said, "Ye shall keep My Sabbaths, and reverence My Sanctuary." [2]

To all this reasoning the Puritans objected strenuously, though with great inconsistency, as being themselves sticklers for their own self-appointed fast-days, and their own severe and unscriptural view of the Sabbath. In 1644 the Puritan Parliament passed an ordinance strictly forbidding the observance of all holy days, and appointed a solemn fast to be held on Christmas Day, alleging that that festival was originally of heathen origin. The law required every one to go to work, and that every keeper of a closed shop should be brought before the judge and punished. This condition of things lasted for sixteen years.

Referring to one of the petty objections of the Puritan party to the proper day for the observance of Easter, Dr. Samuel Seabury in his valuable treatise on "The Church Calendar" says, "On such occasions, and even in anticipation of them, the Puritans, whom God seems to have created to try the patience of the saints, were seized with inward spasms." "They were a class of men," he adds, "who stood more in need, as Dr. South somewhere says, of Luke the Physician than of Luke the Evangelist." [3] The Late Bishop Huntington of Central New York, himself of devout Puritan ancestry, expressed a similar opinion when he described Puritanism in this aspect of its character as "a disturbed biliary duct."

If Puritan objections had been confined to the abuse

[1] p. 497.   [2] Ex. iii, 5; Lev. xix. 20.   [3] Pp. 114, 116.

of the Christian Year, to the multiplication of saints' days and other festivals, and to many superstitious practices that had grown up about their observance, they would have been listened to respectfully. We know that the very best of customs are liable to abuse, and have been abused. In fact these very Puritans turned the Lord's Day into a very different kind of day from God's appointment of it; burdensome, hard, and unlovely, very unlike that "delight" which Isaiah says it was meant to be.[1] That, however, is a poor reason for their descendants in this generation making it a day of revelry such as many Church people also, alas, both in England and elsewhere had done, and are doing to-day. So too of Christmas and other holy days. All had been abused, just as similar days among the Jews had been. Isaiah had told the people in the Name of God: "The new moons and sabbaths I cannot away with. It is iniquity, even the solemn meeting."[2] The same was true of their sacrifices and their incense, all of them nevertheless of divine obligation. But perversion and abuse are grounds for destruction only to fanatics, and not to true reformers. All good things have been abused, the Bible, the Prayer Book, the ministry, the sacraments, the altar, the pulpit, the church. The Sabbath was woefully perverted in our Lord's day, but that only gave Him reason for restoring it to its rightful place, not for repealing the law that ordained it.[3]

Even in Apostolic days Jews who had become Christians had to be warned against the perversion of such good customs as they had inherited from their forefathers. "Ye observe days, and months, and times, and years," writes S. Paul to the Jewish Christians of Galatia. "I am afraid of you," he adds, "lest I have

[1] Isaiah lviii. 13.   [2] Isaiah, i. 13.   [3] S. Matt. xii. 8.

bestowed upon you labor in vain."[1] Their old purely Jewish customs were no longer necessary for Christians. They were only "shadows" and "beggarly rudiments," he says.[2] They could indeed lawfully use them, as he himself did, but not impose them as of necessity. All Christian Jews kept Saturday, their old day for keeping the Sabbath, as well as Sunday. We find the Apostle himself on one occasion offering the ancient Jewish sacrifices in the Temple,[3] and this was twenty-five years after his conversion. But all these things had ceased to be of obligation to Jewish Christians, and were purely voluntary.[4] "The body is of Christ."[5] Here is the reality, in feast, and ministry, and sacrament, for which all these "shadows" had prepared the way.

[1] Gal. iv. 10, 11.
[2] Heb. x. 1; Gal. iv. 9, Rev. Ver.
[3] Acts xxi. 20-27.
[4] See Col. ii. 16; Rom. xiv. 4, 5, 6.
[5] Col. ii. 17.

CHAPTER III

THE CHURCH YEAR A GROWTH

"There shall come forth a shoot out of the stock of Jesse, and a branch out of His roots shall bear fruit."—*Isaiah* ii. 1., *Rev. Ver.*

As we proceed to examine the system of the Church's Year we shall see that it is not a completely developed plan from the beginning, but a growth or evolution from a single root, to which many nations and many generations have contributed their special gifts, just as the soil does to the vine. It had its "root" in the ritual year of the Church of Israel. It had its "Branch" in the Incarnate Life of our Lord out of "the root of Jesse."[1] He is the Alpha and the Omega, the Beginning and the Ending, the First and the Last, the Light and the Life, of all her worship and her work.

When we trace it historically we find that, just as surely as our modern fruit trees and vines, peach, apple, plum, grape, have been developed from early wild species with less succulent and palatable fruit, so the Christian Year has its origin in the ritual year of the Patriarchs and of Israel. That was the "root" as well as the "shadow." The "Branch" and the "Body" are "of Christ." It is this "mystery of the Holy Incarnation" which the Church by her Christian Year, with marvellous practical wisdom, has planned century after century to illustrate in dramatic form, by season and day, by lesson and prayer, by hymn and

[1] Is. xi. 10.

color, and in well-rounded proportion, for the edification of all her children.

We must not therefore expect a full account of the Church's ritual year in the New Testament. We must be content if we get only glimpses of it here and there, and allusions to what S. Paul calls the "traditions," and "customs," and "ways" of the Church in Apostolic days, which are not to be lightly disregarded by any man calling himself a Christian.[1] Nor must we expect to find the system of the Christian Year fully developed even in the later days of the Primitive Church. Like the liturgy, and Christian architecture, and art, and hymnology, it took on form and beauty by slow degrees century after century; just as beautiful cathedrals and parish churches, with altars, organs, music, painting, sculpture, trained and vested choirs, took the place of a bare room or a burial chamber in the catacombs; or just as some of the same things to-day take the place of a hired hall, or a disused foundry, or an old railway car in an American or Canadian mining town.

Let us first consider in some detail the immediate source and pattern of the Year of the Church of Christ. One of S. Augustine's many epigrammatic sayings was that the Gospel was "latent in the Old Testament, and patent in the New." That, however, is only another way of expressing the great assertion of our Lord that He came "not to destroy the law or the prophets, but to fulfil."[2] And as Christ Himself was the fulfilment of all the foreshadowing and the promises of "The Gospel preached before" in the Old Testament,[3] so His Church is the fulfilment of the Church of Israel.

This organic continuity, as of a tree from its root, is

[1] 2 Thes. ii. 15; iii. 6; 1 Cor. xi. 2, margin, and 16; iv. 17.
[2] S. Matt. v. 17. [3] Gal. iii. 8.

forcibly and beautifully illustrated in those magnificent prophecies in the 52d, 53d, 54th and 60th chapters of Isaiah, where the new and the old are, in the prophet's vision, indistinguishable one from the other, each growing into and blending with the other. The Church of the promised Christ or Messiah is not a different Church, but the fruition, and enlargement, and glorification of the earlier Church of Israel. Though Israel is in the immediate foreground of Isaiah's vision, it is the glorious Church which is to have its new birth on the Day of Pentecost, and its preachers and priests in " all the world," among " all nations," and " unto the end of the world;"[1] it is this great society and " kingdom of God " that the prophet addresses when he exclaims, " Awake, awake; put on thy strength, O Zion, put on thy beautiful garments, O Jerusalem. . . . How beautiful upon the mountains are the feet of him that bringeth good tidings, that publisheth peace." Or again, after describing the sorrows and the shame of the Cross and Passion, he utters the wonderful apostrophe beginning, " Sing, O barren, thou that didst not bear. . . . Enlarge the place of thy tent, and let them stretch forth the curtains of thine habitation. . . . Thy seed shall inherit the Gentiles. . . . O thou afflicted, tossed with tempest, and not comforted, I will lay thy foundation with sapphires. . . . No weapon that is formed against thee shall prosper; and every tongue that shall rise against thee in judgment thou shalt condemn." And once more in the splendid vision of the 60th chapter he exclaims, " Arise, shine, for thy light is come. . . . And the Gentiles shall come to thy light, and kings to the brightness of thy rising." None of these prophecies ever had any fulfilment in the ancient and literal Church of Israel as it stood

[1] S. Mark xvi. 15; S. Matt. xxviii. 19, 20.

alone. But all history proclaims the great vision realized in the Church of Christ, "My Church,"[1] the "Holy Catholic and Apostolic Church" of the creeds.

And again, just as we find all the ancient sacrifices fulfilled in the "one perfect and sufficient sacrifice" of the Cross, so we see its perpetuation and its commemoration in that holy sacrament instituted in the Upper Room out of the very materials of bread and wine which remained over and above from the Paschal feast, the greatest of all the sacrifices of Israel. And again, as we find the Mosaic or Aaronic priesthood in three sacred orders of high priest, priest, and Levite fulfilled in the one great "Apostle and High Priest, Jesus Christ,"[2] so we see this ancient ministry fulfilled in and merging into the new apostleship and priesthood which our Lord Himself ordained to speak and act for Him on earth.[3] The hereditary and physical descent of the sons of Aaron finds its counterpart and fruition in the spiritual descent of the apostolic succession of the three "Orders of Ministers in Christ's Church,—Bishops [or Apostles], Priests, and Deacons."[4] And in like manner we find the ritual year of Israel dying and blending into the dawn of a more glorious year, just as the Jewish Sabbath, on the primal Easter, "began to dawn toward the first day of the week,"[5] telling in unmistakable accents that those things which prophets foresaw, and "kings desired to see," and the whole world languished for,[6] had indeed come at last in all their fulness.

[1] S. Matt. xvi. 18.

[2] Heb. iii. 1.

[3] S. John xx. 21, 22, 23; Acts i. 8; 2 Cor. v. 20; 1 Cor. iv. 1; and compare Mal. iii. 3 with Acts vi. 7.

[4] Preface to Ordinal in the Prayer Book.

[5] S. Matt. xxviii. 1.

[6] S. Luke x. 24; Haggai ii. 7.

THE RITUAL YEAR OF ISRAEL

was to be the first month of the year to them instead of Tishri at the time of the autumnal equinox (September-October).[1]

The lamb was to be carefully chosen on the 10th day of Abib, and on the 14th it was to be killed in sacrifice, roasted, and eaten, with bitter herbs and unleavened bread, the worshippers all standing with robes girded, and staff in hand, tokens of their haste and readiness for the journey that was to give them freedom. The feast was to continue for seven days until the 21st day at even, during which time there was to be no leaven found in all their houses. Hence the name, the **Feast of Unleavened Bread.** Moreover, though there is no explicit statement to that effect, Jewish scholars tell us that the lamb was roasted whole on two wooden spits of pomegranate. Justin Martyr (second century) and Tertullian (third century) tell us that these were passed through the body like a cross. A cup of red wine also, mingled with water, formed part of the sacred supper.[2]

Besides this historic association of the feast, the Passover had also, as did the other great feasts, a character connected with the agricultural life of the people. "A sheaf of the firstfruits of the harvest" is to be brought to the priest, who is to "wave it before the Lord" in thankful token of their dependence upon Him for their care.[3]

Pentecost, the Greek for *Fiftieth*, is the name given by the Grecian Jews, and the Greek versions of Tobit [4] and 2 Maccabees,[5] to the second great feast, which

---

[1] See Ex. xxiii. 4–15; xxxiv. 18.
[2] See Edersheim's *Life and Times of Jesus*, Vol. II., pp. 480–9, for an interesting account of the feast as celebrated by our Lord and His Apostles.
[3] Lev. xxiii. 10, 11.   [4] Tobit ii. 1.   [5] 2 Maccabees xii. 32.

celebrated the giving of the Law from Sinai fifty days after the departure from Egypt.[1] Its original name was the **Feast of Weeks;**[2] also the **Feast of Harvest,** when "two wave loaves of fine flour," the firstfruits of the harvest, are to be offered unto the Lord.[3]

The Feast of Tabernacles was to be held "in the end of the year," on the 15th day of the seventh month (Tishri), when the people were to dwell in tents or booths for seven days in memory of their journey to the land of Promise.[4] Like the other great feasts it was connected also with the harvest, and was called the **Feast of Ingathering.**[5]

On all these great festivals the first day, and the last day, or octave, were to be marked by "a holy convocation," a great act of united worship. A great fast was also prescribed by the divine law, the **Day of Atonement,** to be held on the 10th day of the seventh month (Tishri).[6]

In addition to these festivals and fasts prescribed by the Law of Moses, and ordained by God, there were others of a minor character, such as the **Feast of Trumpets** (the civil **New Year's Day**), the first of Tishri the seventh month,[7] and the **New Moons.**[8] Chief among those established by the authority of the Church were the **Feast of Purim,** and **The Dedication,** or **Feast of Lights.**

Purim was observed on the 14th and 15th of the month Adar (part of December and January). It commemorated the deliverance of the Jews (509 B.C.) during their captivity in Persia, when Haman, the Agagite, plotted

---

[1] Ex. xix., xx. [2] Deut. xvi. 9, 10.
[3] Ex. xxiii. 16; Lev. xxiii. 15, 16, 17.
[4] Lev. xxiii. 34 to end. [5] Ex. xxiii. 16.
[6] See Lev. xvi. and xxiii. 27. Compare Heb. ix. 12, 25.
[7] Lev. xxiii. 24. [8] 1 Sam. xx. 5; Psalm lxxxi. 3, etc.

THE RITUAL YEAR OF ISRAEL 19

to destroy them, and Esther the Queen, a Jewess, by her intercessions delivered them.[1] **The Feast of the Dedication,** or of **Lights,** was held on the 25th of the ninth month, Chisleu (Nov.-Dec.), in memory of the cleansing and rebuilding of the Temple and altar after their desecration by the armies of Antiochus Epiphanes, when the Jews won a great victory over their enemies under the generalship of the patriot Priest, Judas Maccabeus in 166 B.C.[2] Compare S. John x. 22, where our Lord is present at the feast.

Besides the great fast of the Day of Atonement, other fasts were prescribed by ecclesiastical authority. Chief among these was that which commemorated the destruction of the Temple and city by fire, 586 B.C., on the 7th of the fifth month, Ab (July-August).[3] Other fasts in the fourth, seventh, and tenth months are mentioned by Zechariah.[4] The 2d and 5th days of the week (Monday and Thursday) were also fast days.[5]

The names of the months according to the Church Calendar of Israel are as follows: (1) *Abib* or *Nisan*,[6] (corresponding to parts of March and April); (2) *Iyyar* (April-May); (3) *Sivan*[7] (May-June); (4) *Tammuz* (June-July); (5) *Ab* (July-August); (6) *Elul*[8] (August-September); (7) *Tishri* (September-October); (8) *Marchesvan* (October-November); (9) *Chisleu*[9] (November-December); (10) *Tebeth*[10] (December-January); (11) *Shebat*[11] (January-February); (12) *Adar*[12] (February-

---

[1] Esther ix.
[2] 1 Macc. iv. 36 to end.
[3] See 2 Kings xxv. 8, and compare Zech. vii. 3, 4, 5.
[4] Zech. viii. 19.
[5] S. Luke xviii. 12.
[6] Ex. xiii, 4; Neh. ii. 1; Esther iii. 7.
[7] Esther viii. 9.
[10] Esther ii. 16.
[8] Neh. vi. 15.
[11] Zech. i. 7.
[9] Zech. vii. 1: Neh. i. 1.
[12] Esther iii. 7; Ezra vi. 15.

March). Only the names of the first, third, sixth, ninth, tenth, eleventh and twelfth months are found in the Old Testament. None are recorded in the New.

Dr. Edersheim, a clergyman of the Church of England, of Jewish parentage and early education, gives the following vivid picture of the effect of all this system of festival and fast upon the opening mind and imagination of a Jewish child:

"There could not be national history, nor even romance, to compare with that by which a Jewish mother might hold her child entranced. And it was his own history—of his tribe, clan, perhaps family; of the past, indeed, but yet of the present, and still more of the glorious future. Long before he could go to school, or even Synagogue, the private and united prayers and the domestic rites, whether of the weekly Sabbath or of festive seasons, would indelibly impress themselves upon his mind. In midwinter there was the festive illumination in each home. In most houses, the first night only one candle was lit, the next two, and so on to the eighth day; and the child would learn that this was symbolic, and commemorative of the **Dedication of the Temple,** its purgation, and the restoration of its services by the lion-hearted Judas the Maccabee. Next came, in earliest spring, the merry time of **Purim,** the feast of Esther and of Israel's deliverance through her, with its good cheer and boisterous enjoyments. Although the **Passover** might call the rest of the family to Jerusalem, the rigid exclusion of all leaven during the whole week could not pass without its impressions. Then, after the **Feast of Weeks,** came bright summer. But its golden harvest and its rich fruits would remind of the early dedication of the first and best to the Lord, and of those solemn processions in which it was carried up to Jerusalem.

As autumn seared the leaves, the **Feast of the New Year** [**Trumpets**] spoke of the casting up of man's accounts in the great Book of Judgment, and the fixing of destiny for good or for evil. Then followed the Fast of the **Day of Atonement,** with its tremendous solemnities, the memory of which could never fade from mind or imagination; and, last of all, in the week of the **Feast of Tabernacles,** there were the strange leafy booths in which they lived and joyed, keeping their harvest-thanksgiving, and praying and longing for the better harvest of a renewed world."[1]

It was amid such surroundings, and under such influences, that our Lord, and His Apostles, and first disciples, and the first Christians, grew from infancy to manhood and womanhood.

[1] *The Life and Times of Jesus the Messiah,* vol. I, pp. 228, 229.

CHAPTER V

THE JEWISH YEAR AND THE APOSTOLIC CHURCH

"Thus saith the Lord, stand ye in the ways, and see, and ask for the old paths, where is the good way, and walk therein, and ye shall find rest for your souls."—*Jer.* vi. 16.

IN considering the Jewish Year as it affected the religious lives of the early Christians, it is important to remember that it was only part of a great system of what we call churchly ways and customs in which our Lord and His Apostles, and all the first converts, had been trained from childhood. They knew no other kind of religious life. Their buildings for worship, especially their Temple, had not been merely "meeting-houses," but sacred places, "houses of God" and "of prayer."[1] Their worship had not been left to individual taste or haphazard. It was liturgic, dignified, largely musical as rendered by trained and vested choristers, with well-known and accustomed prayers, and a set form and order of service both in Synagogue and Temple. They had been ministered to by a priesthood in three sacred orders, not appointed or instituted by the people, but ordained by the special command and authority of God, so that "no man" dare assume the office, "take this honor unto himself," as the author of the epistle to the Hebrew Christians puts it,[2] but must have the

---
[1] S. Matt. xii. 4; S. John ii. 16. [2] Heb. v. 4.

THE JEWISH YEAR

lawful call of God in His appointed way. These priests and other ministers were accustomed also to wear an official vestment in their public ministrations.

To these customs and traditions our Lord as a true Israelite was supremely loyal. While He was open in His condemnation of hypocrisy and greed in the rulers of the Church, never once was He charged by His enemies with disloyalty to the priesthood itself. While He condemned freely the formalism of the Pharisees and their followers, He was never accused by them of despising or neglecting the Church's solemn worship or her festivals and fasts. He had been brought up in a godly home; admitted as a member of the Church when only eight days old; presented as an offering to God in His Temple when He was only six weeks old.[1] When he was twelve years He was "confirmed," as we might express it, and admitted to all the sacred privileges of the Church, her sacrifices and other ordinances. When thirty He submitted to a form of baptism, "the baptism of repentance,"[2] which had no divine authority, but only the sanction of the later Church of Israel as an appropriate ordinance for receiving converts (proselytes) from heathenism and repentant Jews, the former of course receiving circumcision also.[3] Even to the last day of His life He submitted Himself to all the lawful authority of the priesthood, in spite of the fact that it was the ruling members of this very priesthood who hounded Him to His death.[4] Always and everywhere He was a true Israelite, faithful even in the "mint, anise, and cummin" as well as in "the weightier matters of the

[1] Lev. xii; S. Luke ii. 21–25.
[2] S. Mark. i. 4.
[3] S. Luke ii. 41, 42; S. Matt. iii. 13–16.
[4] S. Luke v. 14; xvii. 14; S. Matt. xxiii. 2, 3.

law"; "in all the commandments and ordinances of the Lord blameless."[1]

But it is perhaps in His loyalty to the ritual year of Israel that we have the most striking illustration of this feature of our Lord's life of "obedience."[2] As we see Him when a boy of twelve careful to observe the feast of the Passover; then sitting at the feet of the doctors in the Temple listening submissively to their teachings; then "subject" to His parents in Nazareth,[3] so we find Him continuing to do even to the close at that last Passover which He glorified by His death and resurrection. Nor were the feasts of divine appointment the only ones which He honored. We find Him keeping at least one which had only the authority of the Church for its observance, the feast of the Dedication, which had been instituted by Judas Maccabeus 200 years before, to commemorate the restoration of the Temple and altar after their desecration by the heathen invaders.[4]

And the most remarkable thing in this connection is the fact that our Lord deliberately made choice of the two greatest feast days of the ancient Church with which to associate the chief events of His life, and of the life of His Church. Let us not forget that the time of His death was wholly in His own keeping. "No man taketh it from Me" He had said of His life; and again He asserted, "My time is not yet full come."[5] And this chosen time and hour of His was the great feast of the Passover. When the day approached He prepared for it in the most exact and careful way.[6] On the very day, and probably at the very hour, when the lamb of the Passover should have been offered up—for in their

---

[1] S. Matt. xxiii. 23; S. Luke i. 6.   [2] Heb. v. 8.
[3] S. Luke ii. 41 to end.   [4] S. John x. 22; 1 Macc. iv. 52–59.
[5] S. John x. 18; vii. 8.   [6] S. Matt. xxvi. 18.

eagerness for His blood the priests seem to have neglected the proper time—at this moment the true "Lamb slain [in intention] from the foundation of the world "[1] was actually offered in sacrifice upon the cross.

And when we come to the next supreme event in our Lord's work for the world, the case is perhaps still more remarkable. During forty days the risen Lord remained on earth to instruct His Apostles how to set about the establishing of His Church, and to give them proofs of the reality of His resurrection.[2] But why, after the forty days were ended, and He had ascended into heaven, did He oblige them to wait ten days longer as "orphans," "comfortless," without His visible presence, and also without the promised Comforter? To us as to them it seems at first incomprehensible that He should not have sent the Holy Ghost at once. But whatever other reason there may have been besides this trial of their faith and patience, the peculiar significance of His *not* sending the Holy Ghost until the feast of Pentecost, the fiftieth day after His resurrection, is beyond a question. Pentecost, coming as it did in the early summer, was doubtless chosen also for the very practical reason that travel by sea and land was then safer and easier, and vast numbers of worshippers from distant countries were then able to come to Jerusalem; "Parthians, and Medes, and Elamites, and the dwellers in Mesopotamia," and all the other foreign Jews who are named by S. Luke in the second chapter of the Acts as being present there on the Church's birthday. Nevertheless it still remains a striking testimony to our Lord's valuation of the ritual year of Israel as an instrument of witness and of popular instruction, that it was not, as S. Luke expresses it, until "the day of Pentecost was

[1] Rev. xiii. 8.   [2] Acts. i. 3.

fully come" that the promised Paraclete came indeed with visible and audible signs to give life and power to the little anxious flock of "about one hundred and twenty" souls[1] who on that day constituted the Holy Catholic and Apostolic Church of Christ.

Our Lord had not told them at what particular time His promise of the Comforter should be fulfilled. They had asked Him when His great work of "restoration of the kingdom" should begin, but His only reply was that they must wait patiently in Jerusalem.[2] Nevertheless they seem to have had some assurance that the day of the next great feast which commemorated the giving of the law from Sinai, and celebrated God's continual care of His people in the gathering of the firstfruits of the harvest, should be the time of His coming. For we are told that on that day they "were all with one accord in one place" in evident expectation.[3]

It was then in such an atmosphere, and with such examples before them, that the Apostles and first Christians were born and bred. Could it be possible, we may well ask, that, under the plea that henceforth the worship of God is to be "in spirit and in truth," they would cast aside as useless or worse all these sacred customs and traditions of their race and Church, so honored by their Lord Himself all His life long? That is the incredible thing which most of the sects of modern Protestantism would have us believe. Was there henceforth to be no sacred order of priesthood in the new Church as there had been in the old, though Christ had taken such pains to train and teach, not only twelve, but seventy men, choosing them and separating them from the multitude and especially commissioning the twelve in the most solemn way, to act for Him on earth "unto

[1] Acts. i. 15. [2] Acts. i. 4–8. [3] Acts ii. 1.

the end of the world"? Were there henceforth to be no ordered worship, no dignified official robes, no ritual year of festival and fast to commemorate the infinitely greater events of those " good tidings of great joy," of which the old feasts and fasts were but the dim foreshadowings? Knowing the atmosphere in which our Lord and His Apostles lived and moved, we are now in a position to see what importance the whole Church in the earliest days would naturally attach to these things as they were developed and carried over into the Church of Christ.

CHAPTER VI

THE BEGINNINGS OF THE CHRISTIAN YEAR IN THE APOSTOLIC CHURCH

"Christ our Passover is sacrificed for us, therefore let us keep the feast."—1 *Cor.* v. 7, 8.

"I must by all means keep this feast that cometh in Jerusalem."—*Acts* xviii. 21.

"He hasted, if it were possible for him, to be at Jerusalem the day of Pentecost."—*Acts* xx. 16.

CONFINING ourselves now to the single question of the ritual year, it would at the outset seem most natural that the first converts, instead of rejecting, would Christianize the old sacred festivals when, as we have seen, they were not only religiously observed by their Lord, but also actually and deliberately connected by Him with the greatest events of His own life and work. Let us see then what glimpses we can get in the New Testament concerning how the Apostles actually regarded these ancient hallowed festivals from the standpoint, not of Judaism, but of the Church of Christ.

1. First of all we find S. Paul, twenty years after the descent of the Holy Ghost, telling his Jewish fellow countrymen in Ephesus, when they urged him to remain longer with them, that he "must by all means keep this feast that cometh [namely, **Pentecost**] in Jerusalem."[1] Four years later we find S. Luke telling concerning him that he "hasted, if it were possible for him, to be at

[1] Acts xviii. 21.

BEGINNINGS OF THE CHRISTIAN YEAR

Jerusalem the day of Pentecost."[1] So too S. Paul himself, in his first letter to the Corinthians, writes, "I will tarry at Ephesus until Pentecost."[2]

Now what was the thought uppermost in the mind of a man like S. Paul in the keeping of this feast of Pentecost? The older reason for its observance, namely, the giving of the law from Sinai and the birth of the Mosaic Church, was doubtless not forgotten. As a Jewish feast the day had still many sacred associations for him, "a Hebrew of the Hebrews."[3] But the new and greater reason for his "keeping the feast" as a Christian lay elsewhere. The marvellous giving of the Holy Ghost on this day some twenty years before, that He might "write the Law on men's hearts,"[4] and gather in the "firstfruits of the harvest"[5] of which our Lord Himself was the chief Sower, and bring to its birth the Church of the new Israel and new Jerusalem—this must have been the dominant thought in the Apostle's mind. It could not have been otherwise.

2. As regards the observance of **Easter** as a Christian festival by the Apostolic Church we have fewer intimations given us in the New Testament. The word occurs only once in our Authorized Version, where it is said of Herod that he "intended after Easter" to put S. Peter to death.[6] But the word here in the original is simply "Pascha" or "Passover," and nothing can be inferred from it concerning the Christian observance of the day. It is very probable, however, that S. Paul is referring to the Christian observance of Easter when, writing to the Church in Corinth concerning a shameful scandal in that Church, he urges them to "purge out the old leaven" of sin, "for," he adds, "Christ our Passover is sacri-

---

[1] Acts xx. 16.   [2] 1 Cor. xvi. 8.   [3] Phil. iii. 5.
[4] Heb. viii. 10.   [5] Ex. xxxiv. 22.   [6] Acts xii. 4.

ficed for us, therefore let us [us Christians] keep the feast." [1]

But however that may be, we know that the time of the Crucifixion and the Resurrection was kept as a great annual feast of the Church from the beginning. In fact so early and so universal was its observance, and so important was it regarded as a witness to the resurrection, that a difference in regard to the proper day for its observance was the occasion of the first schism in in the Church, some Eastern Churches holding that it should be kept on any day of the Paschal week, and others that it should be always on a Sunday as the first Easter had been.[2] This controversy will be explained more in detail later on.[3]

3. And the observance of **Sunday** or "the first day of the week," instead of Saturday which the Jews reckoned as "the seventh," rests upon exactly the same authority as that of Pentecost and Easter, namely, the early and universal custom and tradition of the Church. Here the New Testament is perfectly clear. It is true we have nowhere the record of a command for the change by our Lord, though such a direction may have been given among those "things pertaining to the kingdom of God," that is, the Church, of which He spoke to the Apostles during the great Forty Days between His resurrection and His ascension.[4] But the absence

[1] 1 Cor. v. 7, 8.
[2] S. Mark xvi. 2. [3] See Chapters XII and XX.
[4] Our Lord, so far as we have any record, uses the word "Church" only on two occasions and that in private (S. Matt. xvi. 18; xviii. 17) while He employs the phrase "kingdom of heaven" (S. Matthew only) or "kingdom of God" constantly. In the mouth of the Apostles after the Church is set up this proportion is entirely reversed. "The Church" now becomes the common designation; "the kingdom" uncommon. In the Acts, Epistles, and the Rev-

of such a record makes the change all the more remarkable. Here was a provision, not of the ritual but of the moral law, the Fourth Commandment, requiring six days for labor, and a seventh for rest and worship; and for 1500 years or more the whole nation had been keeping what we call Saturday as the Sabbath. It was therefore most natural that Jews would come to think that Saturday and " the seventh day " must necessarily mean the same thing. To change to another "seventh" day would seem a breach of the moral law itself. But the Church in the New Testament and ever after, until the "Seventh Day Baptists" appeared 1600 years later, never showed the faintest hesitation on the subject. Sunday, or " the first day of the week," was adopted apparently at once as the weekly festival day commemorating and witnessing to the resurrection, just as Easter does as the annual festival day which witnesses to the same fact.

This does not imply that Saturday was no longer observed by Jews who became Christians. It was most natural, and we know it to be the case from early historians, that devout Jewish Christians observed both days, as they also continued to observe other customs of Jewish worship. These, however, were purely voluntary matters with them. They were not to be regarded

---

elation "kingdom" occurs 25 times, "the Church" 111 times. Our Lord's unequal use of the words is easily accounted for by the fact that while it was under the figure of a kingdom that the prophets foretold the new order, "Church," either in Hebrew (Aramaic) or in the Greek of the Septuagint, was the word in common use among the Jews for their present "household of faith." See Acts vii. 38 and Heb. ii. 12. Christ would therefore avoid all unnecessary clashing with Jewish prejudice, and only employs "Church" in speaking privately to His Apostles. But once the Church is set up openly, the day for consulting prejudice is past

as obligatory or perpetual any more than the circumcising of their children, or the rule about "clean" and "unclean" meats, or the offering of the accustomed sacrifices in the Temple while it stood. S. Paul himself, as we have already seen, on one occasion offered sacrifice along with other Christian Jews, and he caused Timothy to receive circumcision even after he became a Christian, in order to meet the prejudices of other Jewish Christians, because though his father was a Gentile his mother was a Jewess.[1]

The observance of "the first day of the week" or Sunday instead of Saturday as the Christian fulfilment of the Fourth Commandment (in which as the primal law there is no trace of Judaism) is evident from the account of the celebration of the Holy Communion on that day in Troas when S. Paul preached, and from the same apostle's direction to the Church in Corinth concerning a special weekly offering on the day for the poor Christians in Jerusalem.[2] It may also be inferred from the account which S. John gives us of the place and the day when he first received his "Revelation." It was "the Lord's Day," he writes, though this might also mean Easter Day.[3]

But all this change of days came very gradually in deference to the very natural prejudices and devout feelings of Jewish converts. The "beggarly elements," as S. Paul calls the old customs and ceremonies of Israel, were allowed to continue for a time, even after the realities of which they were but the shadows and the husk had actually come.[4] The Lord's Day was therefore necessarily slow in supplanting entirely the Saturday Sabbath. In fact the two days continued side by side

[1] Acts xxi. 18, etc.; xvi. 4; Col. ii. 16, 17.
[2] Acts xx. 7; 1 Cor. xvi. 2.   [3] Rev. i. 10.   [4] Gal. iv. 9.

for several centuries as "sister days," as Gregory the Bishop of Nyssa in the fourth century calls them. The Apostolic Constitutions, so-called, which probably represent even an earlier period than the fourth century, have this exhortation: Christians must "gather together especially on the Sabbath, and on the Lord's Day, the day of the Resurrection"[1]; and again they say, "Keep the Sabbath and the Lord's Day as feasts, for the one is the commemoration of the Creation, and the other of the Resurrection."[2] This was a common rule in the East, though curiously enough at Rome the Saturday Sabbath was a fast day in the time of S. Augustine, and the same is true of some other places in the West, though the majority of Western Churches did not so regard it. At Milan, for instance, the day was not treated as a fast; and S. Ambrose, in reply to a question put by Augustine at the instance of his mother Monica, stated that he regarded the matter as one of local discipline, and gave the sensible rule to "do in such matters at Rome as the Romans do."[3]

Another fact to be borne in mind in regard to the observance of Sunday as well as other festivals of the Church in the early days is that, during the first three centuries throughout the Roman Empire, Christianity was an illegal religion (*religio illicita*), and therefore frequently the subject of persecution by the State. Judaism on the other hand was a legal religion, and had its weekly Sabbath, but the Roman law recognized no weekly rest day for other nations. Gentile Christians therefore would naturally feel it doubly difficult to observe the Lord's Day as a complete day of

[1] *Apos. Con.* ii. 59. [2] *Apos. Con.* vii. 23.
[3] *The Church Year and Kalendar*, by Bp. Dowden, p. 8. The quotation from Augustine is from Ep. liv. 3, ad Bonifacium.

rest and worship. This would be particularly true of slaves, who formed the majority of the population in most parts of the Empire, and of the working classes generally. This will probably account for the night service which we have seen at Troas, and may serve as an excuse for the sleep of the young man Eutychus after a day of hard toil either as a slave or a free laborer. (It should be remembered also that the Jewish day began at sunset, and not at midnight.) The day was not a legal holiday until the conversion of the first Christian emperor, Constantine, in the beginning of the fourth century, when toleration was first proclaimed, and Christianity became the religion of the state.[1]

[1] It was in A.D. 321 that Constantine gave leave to the Christian soldiers in his army to be absent from duty in order that they might attend divine service on Sunday. The heathen soldiers had to assemble and offer prayers for the Emperor and his family. At the same time Constantine forbade the law courts to sit on Sunday. See Eusebius, *Vita Const.*, 4. 19, 20; and Sozomen, *His. Eccles.*, i. 18.

CHAPTER VII

THE VALUE OF CUSTOM AND TRADITION IN THE CHURCH

"The keeping or omitting of a Ceremony, in itself considered, is but a small thing; yet the wilful and contemptuous transgression and breaking of a common order and discipline is no small offence before God."—*Preface to the English Prayer Book: Of Ceremonies.*

THERE is nothing strange or unreasonable or unscriptural in this resting of the observance of these festival days merely on custom or tradition, instead of on a recorded command of our Lord or His apostles. It is remarkable, though too often overlooked, how frequently the words "tradition," "custom," and "way," or their equivalents, occur in the New Testament. Three times "The Way" is used as a name or designation of the Church itself.[1] S. Paul in writing to correct certain evils in the Church in Corinth gives as a sufficient reason for some things his own "ways in Christ."[2] As a sufficient argument against another practice in the same Church he writes, "We have no such custom, neither the Churches of God";[3] and he says in the same chapter, "Hold fast the traditions, even as I delivered them unto you."[4] To the Thessalonian Church he says, "Stand fast, and hold the traditions which ye have been taught, whether by word, or our epistle"; and again, "We command you in the name of our Lord Jesus Christ, that ye withdraw yourselves from every brother that walketh

---

[1] Acts xix. 9, 23; xxiv. 14, Rev. Ver.   [2] 1 Cor. iv. 17.
[3] 1 Cor. xi. 16.   [4] 1 Cor. xi. 2, Rev. Ver.

disorderly, and not after the tradition which he received of us." [1]

Few of us realize how much the fulness and richness of our common everyday life is dependent on customs and ways handed on to us and by us by tradition, sometimes written, but far more frequently not written. The characteristic, the most valuable features in fact of families and nations alike are these unwritten customs and traditions. They are things not wrought out by each generation, or each set of individuals for themselves, but are inherited and handed on to others. How much a nation or a family would have to give up, how much poorer it would be, if it abandoned all except what is inscribed in its laws or its records, the things "written in the bond." The great bulk of a nation's customs, the pith and heart of its character, is not found recorded in its histories or literature. It could not be described in words; it could not be transferred to another nation by means of written documents alone. If acquired at all by others, it must be acquired by close contact, almost by a new birth and a new life, an engrafting of one into the other, a suffusion of blood.

Now if one will only give the matter a moment's thought it is evident that very much of the life of the Church must necessarily be of this same description. Even to-day, when missionaries go out to heathen lands, there are a thousand things they teach by word and act and "ways" that could not be conveyed by writing. When S. Columba set sail from Ireland to convert the heathen Picts and Scots he took with him many companions, not all ecclesiastics or teachers or preachers, but living examples of what the Christian faith had done, and therefore could do, for men. The business man

[1] 2 Thess. ii. 15; iii. 6.

knows this when he travels hundreds of miles to have only five minutes' talk with some correspondent. He knows that that five minutes' conversation face to face will accomplish more than whole quires of writing.

And in the Church it is no different. Human nature is alike everywhere. And what a host of such " traditions," "customs," "ways" acquired, not from writings, but from the words and acts of the apostles and first Christian missionaries themselves, must have existed in the early Church, nay, must in a large measure still exist throughout the whole historic Church to-day. Tradition means literally something handed on, like the lighted torch in the torch-race of the ancient Greeks, one runner bearing it to a certain point where it is handed to another and another until the goal is attained. And Christian tradition is simply this lighted torch, handed on in the Church from age to age, from generation to generation.

Of course all traditions in the Church cannot be accepted as binding on the conscience unless they can be shown to represent the mind of Christ and His apostles. They must be tested. Have they been handed on unintermittingly and uncorrupted from the beginning?[1] That

[1] A striking illustration of the force and value of tradition "from the beginning" is seen in the existence of the *Sursum Corda*, "Lift up your hearts," with its response, in every known liturgy in the world except two of no special note, namely, the Syro-Jacobite of S. Chrysostom, and of John of Antioch. (See Scudamore, *Notitia Eucharistica*, p. 523.) That such a very minor feature of the great Eucharistic Service should exist in practically every Church, no matter how widely apart in language, and character, and distance, can only be accounted for on one theory, namely, that the words formed part of the use of the Apostolic Church while still in its infancy in Jerusalem. It could not have been incorporated at any later period any more than the fly could have found its way into the amber at any stage later than the " beginning."

is the test that S. John in his old age applies to them. Living on into the twilight of the Apostolic age, all the companions of his early ministry dead and gone, the last writer of the New Testament harps continually on this one string. This old man eloquent, this " disciple whom Jesus loved," who lay on Jesus' breast and heard His heart beat, tells us that the one practical test of essential and fundamental truth and custom is its continuity, its existence in the Church " from the beginning." "Let that therefore abide in you," he writes, "which ye have heard from the beginning." And again, " This is the commandment, That as ye have heard from the beginning, ye should walk in it." "This is the message that ye have heard from the beginning." [1]

This then is the conclusive test which the Church still applies to many things besides the feast days of the Christian Year. It was on this that the motto of the earliest and greatest of the general councils of the Church, "Let the ancient customs prevail," was based. It is the reason which the Church, in her sixth Article of Religion, gives for claiming our acceptance of the Scriptures themselves. What she says is this: " In the name of the Holy Scripture we do understand those canonical books of the Old and New Testament, of whose authority was never any doubt in the Church." And again in the twentieth Article she declares that the Church is " a witness and a keeper of Holy Writ."

And as it is with the Bible so is it with the Ministry. That too, she asserts, is dependent on the tradition and continuous witness of the Church " from the beginning "; not apart from the witness which Holy Scripture, that other sacred tradition, gives it, but together with it;

[1] 1 John ii. 24; iii. 11; 2 John 6.

THE VALUE OF CUSTOM AND TRADITION 39

a double witness therefore. In the Preface to the Ordinal in the Prayer Book the Church says, " It is evident unto all men, diligently reading Holy Scripture and ancient Authors, that from the Apostles' time there have been these Orders of Ministers in Christ's Church,—Bishops, Priests, and Deacons." That is what tradition "from the beginning" gives us; the tradition concerning the Scriptures, and side by side with it the tradition concerning the Sacred Ministry by Apostolic Succession. The New Testament proves its right to our acceptance to-day because it has been accepted as the authentic teaching of Christ and His apostles and evangelists from very early days; and the Ministry has a still greater claim because it has been "from the beginning," even before a word of the New Testament was written. In fact the complete canon of the books of the New Testament was not formally determined by the Church until the third council of Carthage in A.D. 397; and the final form of the Creed not until the council of Nice in 325; while, by the common consent of all historical scholars, the three-fold Ministry was in existence everywhere in the Church before the martyrdom of S. Ignatius in A.D. 110. Thus the appeal of Holy Scripture to "tradition," "custom," and "ways" is simply what modern scholarship would call the appeal to history.

And what is true of the New Testament and the Ministry is true of many other things. It is for this reason for instance that the Church baptizes infants; admits women to the Holy Communion; requires " the laying on of hands" by a successor of the Apostles for the gift of the Holy Spirit in Confirmation; builds churches after the pattern of the Temple with an altar, and not after the pattern of a synagogue with a mere platform; employs a "form of sound words" for common prayer and confession of belief in public worship; celebrates the Holy Communion as the central act of all our worship on every Lord's Day; has the clergy wear appropriate vestments in divine service; and finally, observes a ritual year of festival and fast, setting forth before the eyes of the world the great foundation truths of the faith as manifested in the life and death of our Lord.

We are not to expect any of these things to be carefully recorded and commanded in the pages of the New Testament. They existed before the New Testament was written. They existed independently of the New Testament, and would have continued to exist if there never had been any New Testament. They are such customs and ways and traditions as those concerning which S. Paul writes to the Church in Corinth and Thessalonica. They are part of that "continuity in the Apostles' doctrine, and fellowship, and the breaking of the bread, and the prayers" which is noted by S. Luke as one of the essential characteristics of the Catholic and Apostolic Church as it came fresh from the hand of God. And the command comes to us equally as to them to "stand fast and hold" these customs and traditions as some of God's best gifts for our spiritual good. We thus see the absurdity of the motto, "The Bible, and the Bible only the religion of Protestants," when it is carried out to its logical limits in the rejection of all traditions. The Bible, itself a great tradition, is the supreme example of the value and the necessity of tradition in the Church "from the beginning."

It will be asked then very naturally, what is the purpose of Holy Scripture if traditions and customs and ways in the Church have such weight? It is well for us to understand very clearly the answer to this question.

THE VALUE OF CUSTOM AND TRADITION 41

"'I believe it to be an error," writes Archbishop Alexander, "to suppose that, as a matter of fact, our first or only knowledge of Christ and of His claim upon us is derived from that sacred volume. I cannot see the faintest indication in the New Testament itself that such a thing was ever contemplated by our Lord or by His apostles."[1] "The Church's earliest mind," writes Canon Scott Holland, "was strongly against writing. Writing was not its most natural method of preserving its story. It distrusted the accidents that beset it, the changes, the blunderings; it disliked the deadness of a dumb document. Our Lord had not written one word [except what He wrote on the dust of the Temple pavement, which the feet of the next passerby blotted out for ever].[2] He had definitely preferred to use living, human memories, written on the tablets of the heart; and the loyal impulses of the Church all set in the channels which He had marked down. Only very slowly, as the pressure of lengthening circumstances compelled her to face new possibilities, was she forced to see the necessity of depositing, in black and white, her witness to the Resurrection. And there can be no more convincing proof of her unwillingness to trust to writing than her own tradition that it was only when the death of the last apostle was ominously near, that S. John could be induced to write down his record."

Dean Hook has summed up this truth very forcibly when he says, "We receive our religion from the Church; we prove our religion from the Bible." Dr. Edward Hawkins, the Provost of Oriel College, says, "The Scriptures themselves presuppose tradition; the New Testament implies a previous acquaintance with the out-

[1] *Primary Convictions*, p. 172.   [2] S. John viii. 6.

line of its doctrines."[1]   And all this is but another form of stating the fact enunciated by S. Luke when he gives the reason for writing the book which is called by his name, and which was at the first meant for the special use of his friend Theophilus. It is, he says, "That thou mightest know the certainty of those things wherein thou hast been instructed," literally " catechized," that is, taught by word of mouth.[2]

[1] *On the Use and Importance of Unauthoritative Tradition*, Oxford, 1819.
[2] S. Luke i. 3, 4.

CHAPTER VIII

THE CHURCH CALENDAR AND ITS USE

> "My Prayer Book is a casket bright,
>   With gold and incense stored,
> Which every day, and every night,
>   I open to the Lord:
> Yet when I first unclasp its lids,
>   I find a bunch of myrrh
> Embalming all our mortal life;
>   The Church's Calendar."
> —*Bishop Coxe, Christian Ballads.*

WE are now in a position to understand the importance of the system which we name the Christian Year. A neglected part of the Prayer Book, yet one of great practical value and historical interest, is the Calendar with its accompanying tables. Before speaking of the feasts and fasts and other holy days into which the Calendar divided the year, I must speak first of the year itself as the early Christians found it in the Greek and Roman cities where they lived. The Greeks and Romans had their own calendars. Under the Greeks the computation of the years was by what were called Olympiads, that is, the intervals between two successive celebrations of the Olympic games. These were terms of four years beginning with what we call the year 776 B.C. (Before Christ). Under the Romans their years were dated from the foundation of their city, *Ab Urbe Condita*, or A.U.C.; which, according to our reckoning, would be 753 B.C.

The years of the Christian era, as we know, are dated from the birth of our Lord, or *Anno Domini*. But we must remember that this method was not adopted by Christians from the very beginning. A moment's thought will show us why. Such a method of reckoning the years would have clashed at once and uselessly with all the business, and social, and governmental life of their day. It is just as if Englishmen had adopted a new method of reckoning the years after the Norman Conquest, dating their time henceforth from A.D. 1066; or as if Americans after the war of the Revolution had made a new beginning of their calendar with the year of the Declaration of Independence, 1776; or, as the French revolutionists actually did when Year 1 was fixed to begin on September 22, 1792, the date of the proclamation of the Republic. It was not until after the year 313, when the empire became nominally Christian, that such a use was possible; and it was not until two centuries later, namely, in the year 541, that the custom was introduced of dating the time from the year of our Lord's birth. This was brought about by the work of a man named Dionysius Exiguus, or The Little, a learned and devout monk, a Scythian by birth, but residing in Rome.

This late date of the adoption of Anno Domini, or "the Year of the Lord," for universal reckoning accounts for an error which we now know crept into the computation. Modern astronomical and historical studies show us that our Lord was born four years earlier than Dionysius supposed, so that January 1, 541, as he numbered it, should have been January 1, 545. This error has never been corrected.

In considering the Church Calendar it is important to remember that a calendar is different from an almanac. An almanac has to be renewed every year. A calendar

THE CHURCH CALENDAR AND ITS USE 45

remains unchanged through all the centuries because it is "a permanent distribution of time on astronomical principles, adapted to civil and secular affairs as well as to religious."[1] It gets its name from a Greek word *kaleo*, signifying "to call." "The first day of the month was named by the ancient Romans the Calends, because on that day the people were called or summoned by the Pontifex into the Curia Calabra, and there informed of the holy days of the [coming] month."[2] The Greeks had no Calends, hence the saying "It will be paid on the Greek Calends," that is, never.

The civil calendar as we have it to-day we owe to the genius of Julius Cæsar. In his time the years were measured by the moon instead of by the sun, the months being literally *moonths*. By this imperfect method, which gave only 355 days to the year, with intercalary days added occasionally by way of correction, summer and winter would in time have changed places, and already the seasons were two months in arrears. With the advice of a learned man, Sosigenes, Cæsar fixed on 365 and a quarter days as the approximately true solar year; one day was added every fourth or "leap" year; the months were given the names and number of days as at present; two months, November and December, were skipped, and what would have been November 1, 45 B.C. was made January 1, 44 B.C., and the beginning of the new or Julian calendar.

But even this Julian year of 365 and a quarter days was only approximately correct, and after sixteen centuries had passed it was found by astronomers that the calendar was again slow by about ten days, so that what was March 11, 1582, was really the day of the vernal equinox, and should have been March 21. It was decreed therefore

[1] Seabury, p. 1. [2] Ib. p. 2.

by Pope Gregory for the Churches in communion with Rome, after consultation with learned men, that October 5, 1582, should be reckoned as October 15. This "New Style" (N.S.), as it was called, was not accepted in England, probably through religious prejudice, until 1752, when the English Parliament abandoned the "Old Style" (O.S.) and adopted the New. By this time the error had increased to nearly twelve days instead of ten, which made Christmas Day of that year (O.S. 1752) to become the feast of the Epiphany (N.S. 1753), and caused the ignorant country folk to complain that they had been robbed of twelve days of their life. For this reason also the Epiphany came to be called by them "Old Christmas." The Greek and Russian Churches still retain the Old Style, but there is at present in Russia a movement to bring about the adoption of the New Style, and so bring the Oriental Churches into accord with the rest of the Christian world.

CHAPTER IX

TECHNICAL WORDS IN THE CALENDAR

"God set the sun and moon for signs:
  The Church His signs doth know,
And here, while sleeps the sluggish world,
  She marks them as they go.
Here for His coming looks she forth
  As for her Spouse the bride;
Here, at her lattice faithfully,
  She waits the morning-tide."
—*Bishop Coxe, Christian Ballads.*

THERE are certain words found in the prefatory portion of the Prayer Book which demand explanation. The first of these is *Cycle*, more fully the *Lunar Cycle*. It is also called the *Metonic Cycle* after its Greek inventor, Meton, who flourished at Athens about the year 432 B.C. This is a term of nineteen years, during which time the sun and moon arrive at the same relative position in the heavens with which they began nineteen years before. "As reduced to more accurate dimensions by the Alexandrian Bishops,"[1] it is still used to find the correct time for the observance of Easter, which varies from year to year, being dependent, as we shall see later, on the age of the moon at the time of the vernal equinox (March 21st). Though the Metonic Cycle is not mathematically perfect it is so nearly so that, with the present provisions of the Gregorian Calendar, the error "will not amount to a day before the year 5200, when it will be only necessary, by an exception to the

[1] Seabury, *Theory and Use of the Church Calendar*, p. 105.

Gregorian rule, to take the year 5200 for a common year instead of a leap year to make our accounts as even as they were before."[1] The Jewish cycle was a period of eighty-four years, but after the Council of Nice, A.D. 325, when the Metonic Cycle was adopted by the Church, the Jews followed the example of Christians.

Another word is the *Golden Number*. This represents the number of the year (1st to 19th) since the beginning of the Lunar Cycle. It is used in the Calendar to designate the day of the full Paschal or Easter moon. These Golden Numbers are printed in the first column of the Calendar between March 21st and April 18th, being that portion of the year *after* which (March 22d to April 25th) Easter can alone fall. "In our Church Calendar the Golden Numbers are also called the *Primes;* probably because they serve to indicate the *prime*, a word which was formerly used to signify the *new moon*, but which in this sense is now obsolete."[2] The rule for finding the Golden Number is given under "Tables and Rules, etc.," in the Prayer Book. The origin of the term is said to be that the Athenians were so rejoiced over the discovery of Meton that they caused an account of the cycle to be engraved on tablets of brass with the numbers in gold letters.

The *Epact* is used to designate the age of the moon on the first day of January. Supposing a new moon to occur on January 1st, the new moon on the following January 1st would be eleven days old, because the lunar year of twelve lunar months contains only 355 days, whereas the solar year contains 365 and a quarter days. *Epact* is derived from a Greek word which means to *add*, because it designates the number of days (one to eleven) which must be added to the lunar year to make

[1] Seabury, p. 120. [2] Ib. p. 90.

the time equal to the solar year. The word is still used in the English Church Calendar, but was dropped in the American.

Still another technical word of the Church Calendar is the *Dominical* or *Sunday Letter*. The purpose of this is to designate, as the word implies, the *Dominical* or Lord's Days (*Dies Domini*) in any particular year. It will be observed that, beginning with the first of January and continuing throughout the year, every day of every week has one letter of the alphabet from A to g, appended to it, the first day of the year being always A. When we know the Dominical or Sunday Letter for any particular year, then by means of the Calendar we can tell, without reference to an almanac, what day of the week is represented by any stated day of the year. (The rule for finding the Dominical Letter is given under "General Tables" in the Prayer Book.) Indeed, knowing the Dominical Letter for the year one can determine the day of the week for any stated day of the year without the use of the Calendar by remembering that the first day of each of the twelve months has an unchanging letter in the following order: A (Jan. 1st), d, d, g, b, e, g, c, f, A, d, f. "To assist him in doing so is the design of the following catch lines; which consist of twelve words answering in their order to the twelve months of the year, the first letter of each word being the proper letter for the first day of the corresponding month:

"At Dover Dwells George Brown Esquire,
Good Christopher Finch And David Fryar." [1]

An explanation of the term *Leap Year* is given in a rubric of the Prayer Book of Queen Elizabeth's reign as follows: "When the years of our Lord can be divided

[1] Seabury, p. 33.

into four equal parts [that is, when a given year can be divided by four without a remainder], then the Sunday letter *leapeth*."[1] This means that when the *bissextus dies*, or intercalary day (29th), is added to February, the Sunday or Dominical Letter, which for the first two months may be *D*, is now changed to *C* for the remainder of the year. Another explanation is that the remaining days of the year *leap over* the 29th, that is, take no account of it, so as not to disarrange the letters for the rest of the year. For this reason February 29th has no letter given it in the English Calendar, and in the American it borrows the letter *d* of the day following.[2]

The word *Bissextile* (Latin for *twice sixth*), which is another name for Leap Year, is sometimes, though erroneously, supposed to be derived from the *two sixes* in the number of days in every Leap Year (366). The real origin of the word is this: The 24th of February in the old calendars was called, according to the ancient Roman use, the *sextus dies*, that is, the sixth day before the calends of March, with *f* for its proper letter, as it is to-day. In leap years, however, instead of inserting the intercalary day, as now, after the 28th, it was placed immediately after the 24th, and was also given the letter *f*, thus leaving the letters for the rest of the year unchanged. For this reason it was called the *bissextus dies*, or the *twice* sixth day, and so gave its name to the year.

An exception to the rule for finding the Leap Year is that all years exactly divisible by 100, but not by 400, are *not* leap years. For example, A.D. 1900 was not a Leap Year, but A.D. 2000 will be.

The word *Ferial*, though not used in the Prayer Books

---

[1] Seabury, p. 38.
[2] See "*A Table to find the Dominical or Sunday Letter*," in the Prayer Book.

TECHNICAL WORDS IN THE CALENDAR 51

of the Anglican Communion, in ecclesiastical language designates an ordinary week-day in contradistinction to a *festal* day. "The names most commonly given to the days of the week in the service-books and other ecclesiastical records are 'Dies Dominica' (rarely 'Dominicus') for the Lord's Day, or Sunday; 'Feria II' for Monday; 'Feria III' for Tuesday, and so on to Saturday which (with rare exceptions) is not Feria VII but 'Sabbatum.'"[1] "The astrological names for the days of the week, as of the Sun, of the Moon, of Mercury, etc., were generally avoided by Christians."[2] It is noteworthy that the Portuguese still retain the ancient numerical names for the days of the week, as *segunda feira* or second week-day, *terça feira* or third week-day, etc.

A *Vigil*, the Latin for *watchful*, is the eve or even of certain feast days, and is always a fast or day of abstinence. Only the following days have vigils in the Anglican Communion: Christmas, The Purification, The Annunciation, Easter-Day, Ascension-Day, Pentecost, S. Matthias, S. John Baptist, S. Peter, S. James, S. Bartholomew, S. Matthew, SS. Simon and Jude, S. Andrew, S. Thomas, All Saints. The vigils were omitted in the American revision of 1789, but were retained in the revision of the Church of Ireland in 1870.

Octave (literally *eighth*) signifies the eighth day after a festival. The intervening days are said to be "of" or "within" the octave. The octave had its origin among the Jews.[3] One purpose, doubtless, of prolonging the time in Israel was on account of the risk of error in the date of the great festivals, when most of the worshippers came to Jerusalem from a great distance.

[1] Bp. Dowden, p. 9.   [2] Ib. p. 10.
[3] See Lev. xxiii. 36; Num. xxix. 35; 1 Kings. viii. 65, 66; 2 Chron. xxix. 17; xxx. 22; S. John. vii. 37.

The Immovable Feasts are those which, like Christmas, Circumcision, Epiphany, and the Saints' Days, have a fixed day in the Calendar. *The Movable Feasts* are those which are dependent on Easter, whose date follows the movements of the moon rather than of the sun.

CHAPTER X

THE BEGINNING OF THE YEAR—ADVENT AND CHRISTMAS

> "All time is hers, and, at its end,
>   Her Lord shall come with more,
> As one for whom all time was made
>   Thus guardeth she her store;
> And, doating o'er her letters old,
>   As pores the wife bereft,
> Thus daily reads the Bride of Christ
>   Each message He hath left."
> —*Bishop Coxe, Christian Ballads.*

WHEN we come to examine the calendars of the different national Churches throughout the world—Greek, Roman, Armenian, Russian, Coptic, English, etc.,—we find great variety in their details. Nevertheless, all have one central principle, namely the manifestation of the life of our Lord, from His Incarnation onward through His Passion, Resurrection, Ascension, and His sending of the Holy Ghost. These general features are common to all, and may be considered under three heads, namely, Christmas, Easter, and Pentecost or Whitsunday. Under a fourth head we may consider the Saints' Days as illustrating some of the ripe results and fruitage of the Incarnate Life.

Of the three great feasts which form the framework of the Christian Year in every calendar, we must remember that they correspond, in their historical character, and in their spiritual significance, to the three great feasts of the earlier Church which, in God's providence and purpose, was a shadow of, as well as a preparation for, the great realities that were to come after.[1] They correspond also in a general way in the time of their observance; Christmas to the feast of Tabernacles "in the end of the year"; Easter to the Passover in the spring; Whitsunday to Pentecost in the early summer.

1. "The Nativity of our Lord, or the Birthday of Christ, commonly called **Christmas Day**," is naturally the first subject of our thought. But before considering it we must notice the season of **Advent,** which means *coming*. This is but the period of preparation for Christmas, and therefore marks the beginning of the Church's Year. All the great feasts of the Church have these times of preparation on the natural principle that the mind must be fitted beforehand to grasp the marvellous mysteries which the great feasts commemorate. Advent, however, is not a fast like Lent, but is a time of solemn and penitential thought. "Advent Sunday is always the nearest Sunday to the Feast of S. Andrew, whether before or after."[2] The Scottish Prayer Book of 1637 adds the words, "or that Sunday which falleth upon any day from the 27th of November to the 3d of December inclusively," thus providing for the case of Advent Sunday falling on S. Andrew's Day itself (Nov. 30th).

Our record of the observance of Advent does not go back further than the fourth century. The Roman use under Gregory the Great at the end of the sixth century (A.D. 597), when Augustine landed in Kent to help convert the Anglo-Saxons, included four Sundays in Advent.

As regards the common name for the feast of the

[1] Col. ii. 17; Heb. x. 1.
[2] *Tables and Rules for the Movable and Immovable Feasts.*

BEGINNING OF THE CHURCH YEAR

Nativity our English-speaking Church seems to be peculiar. The Dutch name, *Kersmis*, is the only one that corresponds to it. Both mean of course the Mass of Christ, a word (in Latin *Missa*) which, whatever its origin, was applied to many services in the fourth century, and which came to be applied, though not exclusively, to the Holy Communion in the sixth and seventh centuries.[1] The word is analogous to such popular English terms as Michaelmas for the feast of S. Michael and All Angels; Lammas for the first of August, and Candlemas for the Purification. The names for the day among peoples of the Latin and Celtic races are corruptions of the Latin *Natale*, e.g., the French *Noel*, and the Welsh *Nadolig*. The German name *Weinachtsfest* has reference to the solemn vigils before the festival. The Scandinavian *Yule* is from the old heathen festival at that time of the year.[2]

The early observance of Christmas cannot be so distinctly traced as that of the other greatest festivals. "At Rome, however, Hippolytus (Bishop of Portus, near Rome), at the beginning of the third century, in his Commentary on Daniel [3] fixes the date as Wednesday the 25th of December, in the forty-second year of the Emperor Augustus."[4] S. Clemens of Alexandria, who died little more than a century after the death of S. John, speaks of its observance, while S. Chrysostom, the Bishop of Constantinople in the fourth century, describes it even then as of great antiquity.[5] In a letter he mentions that Julius I, Bishop of Rome from A.D. 337 to 352, had caused a strict examination of the Imperial records of the Roman census taken at the time

[1] See *Heortology*, p. 432.
[2] *Prayer Book Commentary*, S.P.C.K., p. 17.
[3] iv. 23.   [4] Duchesne, p. 258.   [5] *Hom. in Nat. I.*

of our Lord's birth,[1] and as a result confirmed its observance on December 25th.

Throughout the East, the 6th of January was the day when *three* events of our Lord's life were commemorated, namely, His birth, the adoration of the Magi, and His baptism. "It is thus clear," writes Duchesne, "that towards the end of the third century the custom of celebrating the birthday of Christ had spread throughout the whole Church, but it was not observed everywhere on the same day. In the West the 25th of December was chosen, in the East the 6th of January. The two customs, distinct at first, were finally both adopted, so that the two festivals were universally observed, or almost so."[2] The Armenian Church, alone in Christendom, has retained the old date (January 6th) to the present day.

Furthermore, there is a remarkable spiritual significance in the fact that, whether the exact date be correct or not, Christmas stands in the place of the ancient feast of Tabernacles, the great and joyous time of thanksgiving, when the people lived in booths or tents for eight days in remembrance of God's care of them during their journeyings forty years in the Wilderness.[3] So, too, S. John tells us, "The Word was made flesh and *tabernacled among us*."[4]

It is sometimes asserted that the Roman Church was influenced in fixing on December 25th for the purpose of turning away the faithful from the excesses of the ancient pagan festival of the Saturnalia by diverting their thoughts to our Lord's Nativity. But as the Saturnalia began on December 17th and ended on the 23d this theory must

[1] S. Luke, ii. 1.   [2] Duchesne, p. 260.
[3] Lev. xxiii. 33 to end.
[4] S. John i. 14, Rev. Ver. margin. Compare 2 Peter i. 13, 14.

BEGINNING OF THE CHURCH YEAR 57

be discarded. "A better explanation," Duchesne says, "is that based on the [pagan] festival of the *Natalis Invicti*. . . . The Invictus is the Sun, whose birth coincides with the winter solstice, that is, with the 25th of December, according to the Roman Calendar."[1]

And if this be the true date (as there is great probability), it is very significant that it is the third day after the true winter solstice (December 22d) when the sun, after reaching the lowest point on the horizon, begins to ascend and to bring back light and life to a darkened and dying world. So also Christ, "the Light of the World," "the Sun of Righteousness, arises with healing in His wings."[2] There is surely in this nothing incredible, but rather the contrary, when we remember that the Child who was born in Bethlehem of the Blessed Virgin Mary, "in the winter wild," was He by whom this visible earth and sun and moon and stars were made, and "without whom was not anything made that was made."[3] All that we call "Nature" is His. It was "*His* star in the East,"[4] and under His guidance, that led the Wise Men to His cradle; it was His moon, "the faithful witness in heaven,"[5] that pointed to the day of His great sacrifice; and it was His sun that "hid as it were its face from Him,"[6] in sympathy with His dying agonies on the cross. Even in these ways "the heavens declare the glory of God and the firmament showeth His handiwork."[7]

[1] Duchesne, p. 261.
[2] S. John viii. 12; Mal. iv. 2.
[3] S. John i. 3.
[4] S. Matt. ii. 2.
[5] Psalm lxxxix. 36.
[6] Is. liii. 3.
[7] Ps. xix. 1.

CHAPTER XI

OTHER IMMOVABLE FEASTS OF OUR LORD

> "This little index of thy life,
>   Thou, all thy life, shalt find
> So teaching thee to tell thy days,
>   That wisdom thou mayst mind.
> Oh live thou by the Calendar,
>   And when each morn you kneel,
> Note how the numbered days go by,
>   Like spokes in Time's swift wheel."
> *Bishop Coxe, Christian Ballads.*

OTHER Immovable Feasts of our Lord depending on Christmas as their centre are: the Circumcision, on January 1st; the Epiphany, on January 6th; the Presentation of Christ in the Temple, commonly called the Purification of Saint Mary the Virgin, on February 2d; and the Annunciation of the Blessed Virgin Mary on March 25th. The Transfiguration of Christ on August 6th, though a feast of our Lord, can scarcely be said to depend on the date of Christ's birth. Its selection is somewhat, if not wholly, arbitrary.

The **Circumcision** is observed by all Christendom one week after the Nativity (January 1st), except by the Armenian Church, which of course places it on January 13th, January 6th being their Christmas. Originally the day was observed only as the octave of the Nativity, and we learn from the sermons of S. Augustine [1] that in his time the Church kept it as a solemn fast, in protest against the "diabolical feast" of the pagans on that first

[1] *Ser.* 197, 198.

day of the year with its licentious revelry. When these heathen practices gradually ceased, its festal character as the octave of Christmas was restored to the day, and the admission of the Holy Child when eight days old to the privileges of membership in the Church of Israel became the central feature of its celebration.[1] Keble in the opening verse of his poem for the festival notes this combined tone of sadness and joy:

> "The year begins with Thee,
> And Thou beginn'st with woe,
> To let the world of sinners see
> That blood for sin must flow."
> —*The Christian Year.*

It should also be remembered concerning this feast that it is the day on which the Holy Child received the Name declared by the angel,[2] the "Name which is above every name," and to which "every knee should bow."[3] A "black-letter" day to commemorate this event occurs in the present English Calendar, called **Name of Jesus,** but in Saxon times it was observed on the Feast of the Circumcision, and later, on the Second Sunday after Epiphany.

In days when this holy Name is often treated so lightly and irreverently it should not be forgotten that, since the time of the Arian heresy in the fourth century, when our Lord's true nature as perfect God as well as perfect Man was so fiercely assailed, it has been a custom in the Church to show outward reverence for this Name by bowing at its utterance in the Creed and elsewhere. It is simply in recognition of this ancient custom that the Church of England ordains in her canons: "When in time of Divine Service the Lord Jesus shall be men-

[1] S. Luke ii. 21.
[2] S. Matt. i. 21.   [3] Phil. ii. 9, 10.

tioned, due and lowly reverence shall be done by all persons present, *as it hath been accustomed.*" In this connection also S. Paul's custom is surely one to be followed. He never uses the Name casually. It is worthy of remembrance that out of 591 times that S. Paul refers to our Lord in his epistles (including Hebrews) "Jesus Christ" occurs 61 times; "Christ Jesus," 46 times; "The Lord Jesus," 18 times; "Jesus our Lord," 9 times; "Jesus Christ our Lord," 8 times; "Lord Jesus Christ," 68 times; "The Lord," 133 times; "Christ," 227 times, and only in 21 instances does he use the word "Jesus" alone, always with some special reason, as in Phil. ii. 10. In every other instance he adds or employs some word of honor as "Lord" or "Christ" either as prefix or affix.

Another name for the **Epiphany** (Jan. 6th) in the East is the *Theophany*. Epiphany is the Greek word for "Manifestation"; Theophany signifies the "Manifestation of God." This idea was chiefly connected with the first three occasions when "Jesus manifested forth His glory"; *to the Gentiles* when the Wise Men were led by "His star" to His cradle, and "worshipped Him"; *to the Jews* when He was baptized in Jordan, and the Voice came from heaven saying, "Thou art My beloved Son, in whom I am well pleased"; *to His own family and disciples* when He wrought His first miracle in Cana of Galilee.[1] The feast was universally observed in the fourth century, the East making the manifestation of Our Lord's Godhead at His Baptism the dominant thought, and the West laying the chief stress on the visit and adoration of the Magi, so that here the day was commonly designated the **Feast of the Three Kings.** In the East it is still known as the **Feast of Lights** on account

[1] S. Matt. ii. 1-13; S. Mark i. 11; S. John ii. 1-12.

OTHER IMMOVABLE FEASTS OF OUR LORD 61

of its connection with the Baptism of our Lord, baptism being called by the Greeks " the Illumination."

> "Did not the Gentile Church find grace,
> Our mother dear, this favored day?
> With gold and myrrh she sought Thy face,
> Nor didst Thou turn Thy face away."
> —*Keble, Christian Year.*

The number of Sundays after the Epiphany depends on the date of Easter. When Easter falls on one of the earliest days, March 22d, 23d, or 24th, there is only one Sunday after the Epiphany; when it falls on one of its latest days, April 22d, 23d, 24th, 25th, there are six Sundays.

"**The Presentation of Christ in the Temple,** commonly called **the Purification of Saint Mary the Virgin**" (Feb. 2d) was first known, both in the West and in the East, by the Greek name, "*Hypapante*" or "The Meeting," that is, the meeting of Simeon and Anna with Mary and her Child in the Temple.[1] This event, like that of the Circumcision, is another instance of the devout obedience of Mary and Joseph in fulfilling every ordinance of God in His Church.[2] The presentation was to be made when the Child was six weeks old, which fixes the day of the festival on February 2d. Though known better by its popular name of "**The Purification,**" the day is rather a feast of our Lord than of the Blessed Virgin. The Church of Rome, according to Duchesne, appears to have observed no festival of the Virgin, in fact, until the seventh century. **Candlemas,** the other popular English name for the day, had its origin in the early custom of carrying candles in procession as part of the ritual of the feast. This is supposed to have its

[1] S. Luke ii. 22–39.   [2] Lev. xii.

suggestion in the words of Simeon to the Holy Child, "A light to lighten the Gentiles."[1]

The Annunciation (March 25th) is really a feast of our Lord, and not merely of His Virgin Mother. It was already well established in the Church in the seventh century, according to Duchesne. As commemorating the actual Incarnation of Christ the date was placed just nine months before His Nativity. For this reason also it was reckoned in England and some other countries as the beginning of the civil year. This custom began to prevail in England in the twelfth century, and continued to be generally followed till the reformation of the Calendar by Parliament in 1752. The popular English name for the festival is Lady-day, regarding it as in honor of the Blessed Virgin, "Our Lady."

> " 'Twas on the day when England's Church of yore
> Hail'd the new year—a day to angels known,
> Since holy Gabriel to meek Mary bore
> The presence-token of the Incarnate Son."
> —*Keble, Lyra Apostolica.*

Another feast of our Lord is the **Transfiguration** (August 6th). In the present English calendar by an unaccountable omission of the revisers, this has only a secondary place as a "black-letter" day. No special service was provided for it, though it had its own Epistle and Gospel in the Use of Sarum, or Salisbury. At the revision of the Prayer Book in 1892 the American Church, feeling that the great importance of this event in our Lord's life justified and demanded for it a higher position, made it a "red-letter" day, and provided it with proper Lessons, Collect, Epistle, and Gospel.

[1] S. Luke ii. 32.

"Lord, it is good for us to be
 Entranced, enwrapt, alone with Thee;
 And watch Thy glistering raiment glow
 Whiter than Hermon's whitest snow,
 The human lineaments that shine
 Irradiant with a Light Divine:
 Till we too change from grace to grace,
 Gazing on that transfigured Face."

—*A. P. Stanley.*

CHAPTER XII

THE MOVABLE FEASTS—EASTER AND ASCENSION DAY

"'Welcome, happy morning!' age to age shall say,
Hell to-day is vanquish'd, heav'n is won to-day."
—*V. Fortunatus, Trans. J. Ellerton.*

THE purpose and origin of **Easter** have already been considered to some extent in Chapters IV and V.[1] Its connection with the Jewish Passover shows us why the day is not observed as an immovable feast, like Christmas, fixed to a particular month and day of the solar year. On the contrary it is dependent on the varying position of the moon at the time of the vernal equinox (March 21st). This historical association of 3400 years is the reason for the Church insisting on the retention of the ancient Jewish rule for its observance. For Easter, including of course the events of Good Friday, which is the real Passover, is not only the direct successor of the Jewish festival of Unleavened Bread, but represents its complete spiritual fulfilment. The Paschal Lamb slain and offered in sacrifice, then roasted and transfixed upon a wooden cross or spit, without the breaking of a bone; followed by the escape of the Israelites from the angel of destruction, and from the slavery of Egypt through the Red Sea water, all this was the shadow of the true "Lamb of God that taketh away the sins of the world," sacrificed on the wood of the Cross,

[1] For the **Christian observance of the Lord's Day**, or Sunday, see Chapter **VI**.

burnt up with His awful agony and feverish thirst, yet "not a bone of Him broken," and all followed by the mighty deliverance from the bondage of death in the sealed sepulchre of Joseph's garden.

The word *Easter* is peculiar to the Teutonic and Scandinavian nations. The Anglo-Saxon name for April was Eostur-monath, after the goddess Eostre. Hence the German *Ostera*. The Latin and Greek *Pascha* follows the Hebrew *Pesach* or Passover, and the French *Pâques* has the same origin.

The correct form of the English name, it should be observed, is *Easter-Day*, as in the Prayer Book, and not Easter-Sunday, inasmuch as the day is a Sunday necessarily. This recalls the great importance which the early Church attached to the day itself. A discussion arose in the Church about the year 136 as to whether the feast should be kept on the same day as the Jews kept it, namely the 14th day of the month Nisan, no matter on what day of the week it chanced to fall, or else on the Sunday following. Those who insisted on the 14th Nisan were called Quartodecimans, from the Latin word for fourteen. This rule was followed chiefly or solely by Eastern Christians, especially in the region of Ephesus, where it was claimed that it was the custom of S. John. The Western Churches, however, held that the better day was the Sunday following the full Paschal moon, that being the day of the week which our Lord Himself had sanctified by His rising from the dead.

The intense feeling which this controversy occasioned about a thing so apparently trifling, testifies to the vast practical importance which the early Church attached to the day as a witness to the historic reality of the Resurrection. On this single fact, they knew, rested all else of Christian faith, for if Christ's body never rose from the dead their faith in Him was all in vain.[1] It is owing to this fact also that the Eastern Church gave, and still gives, to the day the name "The Feast," as that which outranks all others, and that the Western Church regards it as "The Queen of Festivals."

This feeling in fact was so great that for a time a schism between the Eastern and the Western Churches seemed imminent. When Polycrates, Bishop of Ephesus at the close of the second century, in behalf of himself and the other Bishops of Asia, wrote to Victor, the then Bishop of Rome, defending the tradition of the East, Victor, writes Eusebius the historian, "forthwith endeavored to cut off the Churches of all Asia, together with the neighboring Churches, as heterodox, from the common unity." The Bishops of the West were not in sympathy with Victor in this extreme position, though agreeing with him that Easter should be kept on the Lord's Day, and Irenæus, the famous Bishop of Lyons, in the name of the Church of Gaul, wrote to him in expostulation. He reminds him that "when the blessed Polycarp went to Rome in the time of Anicetus [his predecessor] and they had a little difference among themselves likewise respecting other matters, they immediately were reconciled, not disputing much with one another on this head, . . . and they separated from each other in peace, all the Church being at peace; both those that observed [Easter on Sunday], and those that did not observe [it], maintaining peace."[2] These wise, broadminded words of Irenæus (whose Greek name signifies "Peaceful"), in opposition to the ill-judged zeal of Victor, are of value as applicable to other matters besides the proper day for celebrating our Lord's Resurrection. The

[1] See Rom. i. 4; 1 Cor. xv. 14–20.
[2] Eusebius, *H. E.*, chap. 23, 24.

THE MOVABLE FEASTS—EASTER, ETC. 67

result was that the Asiatic Churches were left undisturbed in their traditional usages, but it is evident that they fell into line with the West sometime before the meeting of the Council of Nice.

And the controversy as to the proper day of the week for observing the feast was not the only difficulty experienced regarding it in the first three centuries. Another was the lack of correct astronomical knowledge as to what was the true Paschal moon, that is, "the full moon which happens upon, or next after, the 21st day of March," which is the vernal equinox.[1]

This difficulty was occasioned by the various imperfect cycles of the moon in use in different countries, the most common being the old Jewish cycle of eighty-four years used by the Roman Church, and the Metonic cycle of nineteen years which the Egyptian Church employed. These questions were finally settled for all time by the great Ecumenical or General Council of Nice in A.D. 325. Then it was decided, among other things, not only that Easter should always be observed on the day of the week on which our Lord rose, namely, the Sunday after the Paschal moon, but also that the fixing of the proper day of the full moon should be left to the Bishop of Alexandria. The city was at this time the greatest seat of learning in the world. Here the Metonic cycle was regarded as that which was nearest perfection, and so it was agreed that, at each preceding Epiphany, the Bishop of that see should give notice of the day to the Bishop of Rome, and through him to all the other Bishops of the Church.[2]

It was this uncertainty as to what was the true cycle

[1] See "Tables and Rules for the Movable and Immovable Feasts."
[2] Seabury, pp. 77, 78.

of the moon that was one occasion of the refusal of the ancient British and Irish Churches to recognize and work with Augustine, whom, in the year 596, Pope Gregory I. had sent to England to help in the conversion of the heathen Anglo-Saxon invaders. On account of the barbarian invasions of the Roman empire in the fifth and sixth centuries, these native Churches had had no intercourse with Rome for a hundred years or more, and meanwhile many changes had taken place in that see. One of these changes was the adoption of the Metonic cycle of Alexandria which Rome had formerly opposed. But being far from the civilization of the Continent, the British and Irish Churches had continued to use the imperfect cycle of eighty-four years employed at first by Rome herself. They were not Quartodecimans, but after a century of lack of intercourse, their reckoning for Easter differed from that of the rest of the Church, and for a long time they stiffly asserted their independence as national Churches by refusing to accept what was really the better rule. This was at length adopted in the south of Ireland about 650; in the north of Ireland in 703; in Scotland in 716; and in South Wales in 802.[1]

All these facts, as I have said, testify to the vast importance which the Church everywhere attached to the right observance of the Easter festival. The whole truth of Christ's claims, and of the religion which He taught, rested on the fact of His actual bodily rising from the dead, and the perpetual and universal celebration of the day was one of the most powerful witnesses to its reality as a fact of history.[2]

Of the observance of **Ascension-Day,** the fortieth day after Easter,[3] we have no mention before the middle

[1] See Prof. Bury's *Life of S. Patrick*, pp. 371-374.
[2] Compare Acts. i. 22; iv. 2, 33; xvii. 18; xxiii. 6.   [3] Acts. i. 3.

of the fourth century. However, in Augustine's time (A.D. 354-430) the observance of the day was universal, and the feast ranked with Easter and Pentecost. A manuscript of a very interesting character in connection with Church usages was discovered in Arezzo in Italy in the year 1884. It is entitled "The Pilgrimage of Silvia," and is dated by scholars at about A.D. 385. It describes a journey to the holy places in Palestine by a devout lady of Gaul "who could read the Fathers in Greek . . . knew the Bible well, and was a very accurate and quick observer."[1] Silvia tells us that in Jerusalem there was a solemn procession on Ascension-Day to the Mount of Olives, where the Empress Helena, who is said to have been born in England, in the city of York, had erected a church as a memorial of the event. Bede, the historian of the English Church in the eighth century, speaks of its celebration as almost as solemn as that of Easter.

Another name for the day in our Prayer Book is **Holy Thursday.**[2] Of the great importance attached by the Church to the bodily ascension of our Lord as witnessing to our own future entrance into Heaven, see the fourth Article of Religion, and the proper preface for Ascension-Day.

[1] Bp. John Wordsworth, *The Ministry of Grace*, p. 57.
[2] See "Other Days of Fasting."

CHAPTER XIII

OTHER MOVABLE FEASTS—WHITSUNDAY AND TRINITY

> "When God of old came down from Heaven,
>   In power and wrath He came;
> Before His feet the clouds were riven,
>   Half darkness and half flame.
>
> "But when He came the second time,
>   He came in power and love,
> Softer than gale at morning prime
>   Hovered His Holy Dove."
> —*Keble, Christian Year.*

WE have already seen how natural it was that **Pentecost** or **Whitsunday** should be observed as a Christian festival from the very earliest day.[1] Its celebration is mentioned by Origen in the third century, and by Gregory Nazianzen and Chrysostom in the fourth. At first the entire fifty days between Easter and Pentecost were observed as a continuous festal season without fasting or kneeling. This early and universal observance of the day could not well have been otherwise considering the previous training of the Apostles and first Christians as devout members of God's ancient Church of Israel.

The coming of the Holy Ghost, the third Person in the Blessed Trinity, resembled the coming of the Eternal Son in that visible and audible signs, the "tongues like as of fire" and the "sound as of a rushing mighty wind," were vouchsafed as sacramental tokens of His presence.

[1] Chapter V.

OTHER MOVABLE FEASTS

Moreover, the day was the birthday of the Church. For just as Christmas had been the birthday of His natural body, so on Pentecost His mystical body, which like the body of Eve had been formed from the pierced side of the second Adam, had breathed into it "the breath of life, and it became a living soul."[1] The associations of the earlier Jewish feast would of course blend with the associations of the Christian festival, especially as "the Feast of Harvest," now fulfilled in the baptism of three thousand believers[2] as "the firstfruits" of the great harvest of risen souls that has been springing up all over the world ever since.[3] But the chief thought in the minds of the Apostles was of course the fulfilment of Christ's promise of "the Comforter" and of "power," without which all their best efforts would be in vain.[4]

Pentecost is the Greek word for *Fiftieth*. It was the name given to the feast by the Grecian Jews before Christ's coming. It is also used in our Prayer Book in "The Table of Fasts." The reference is to the day which closed the seven weeks which elapsed between the Exodus from Egypt and the arrival at Mount Sinai. For this reason it was also called the **Feast of Weeks.** Another name was the **Feast of Harvest** or **Firstfruits**,[5] being held in the early summer, which came naturally much earlier in Palestine than in northern climates.

The name **Whitsunday** (not Whitsun-Day) is peculiar to the English-speaking Church. The original word Pentecost is retained in all Latin countries. Whitsunday is held by some to be a corruption of the German Pfingstentag, but this is more than doubtful. About

[1] Gen. ii. 7.   [2] Acts. ii. 41.   [3] See Chapter V.
[4] S. John xiv. 16, 26; Acts i. 8; Rom. xv. 13.
[5] Ex. xxiii. 16; xxxiv. 22; Deut. xvii. 9.

the year 1200 the English spelling was Hwitesundei, and later Witesoneday, or Wittesonday. The reference may be either to the wearing of white robes by candidates for baptism on the feast, or else to the gift of "*wit*," an old Saxon word for wisdom (as in *witan*, wise man), by the outpouring of the "Spirit of wisdom,"[1] in fulfilment of Christ's promise.[2] The derivation from *white*, however, has strong confirmation in the Welsh, that is, the ancient British, word for the day, namely *Sulgwyn*, gwyn being the Welsh for white.

The name **Trinity Sunday** for the eighth day or octave after Whitsunday is derived from the fact that the revelation of God's nature as Father, Son, and Holy Ghost, which the Church has been unfolding since Advent, is now completed. The festival, therefore, marks the culmination and summing-up of the whole teaching of our Lord as expressed by Him in the formula for Holy Baptism, "the Name of the Father, and of the Son, and of the Holy Ghost"; and later in the Creed of the Church, "I believe in God the Father . . . I believe in His Son Jesus Christ . . . I believe in the Holy Ghost."

The festival is not of an early date. It makes its first appearance in the Low Countries in the tenth century, and makes its way slowly. According to Gervase of Canterbury, the day owes its origin to Thomas Becket, the famous Archbishop of that see from 1162 to 1170. "It was not until the fourteenth century, under the pontificate of John XXII, that the Roman Church received the feast of the Trinity and attached it to the first Sunday after Pentecost."[3] The Eastern Church has no Trinity Sunday, but calls the day "All Holy Martyrs."

[1] Eph. i. 17. [2] S. John xvi. 13.
[3] Dowden, p. 46.

Both the Oriental and the Roman communions count the Sundays "after Pentecost" instead of "after Trinity." In fact the custom of calling the Sundays after Trinity is peculiar to the English-speaking Church, and to those German Churches which were founded by her missionaries. This is noteworthy as a token of the national independence of the British Churches, and also as a witness to their unbroken orthodoxy, inasmuch as the Arian heresy denying the perfect Godhead of our Lord, which so overspread all the rest of the Christian world, never obtained a foothold on British or Irish soil.

In accordance with the early or late date of Easter in any year, the Trinity season may consist of as many as twenty-seven Sundays, or of as few as twenty-two. As there are only twenty-five Collects, Epistles, and Gospels provided for the Sundays after Trinity, the additional Sundays in any year are to be supplied from those omitted in the Epiphany season; provided, however, that the twenty-fifth shall always be used for the Sunday next before Advent.[1]

As the Church Year from Advent to Trinity presents to us step by step the great drama of Redemption, from "the mystery of the Holy Incarnation, the Holy Nativity and Circumcision, the Baptism, Fasting, and Temptation, the Agony and Bloody Sweat, the Cross and Passion, the precious Death and Burial," on to "the glorious Resurrection and Ascension, and the Coming of the Holy Ghost," thus completing the fulness of the revelation of the love and mercy of God in the three sacred Persons of the Holy Trinity; so, for the remainder of the year, the Church presents to us the practical side of the Christian Life as the necessary fruit of such a glorious faith. The Collect, Epistle, and Gospel for the First

[1] See the rubric at the end of the Sunday next before Advent.

Sunday after Trinity, with their thought of "strength" and "weakness," "help" for the "keeping of God's commandments," and the love of God and our brother, or the absence of it, sound the keynote of all the Sundays till we reach Advent once more.

CHAPTER XIV

THE SAINTS' DAYS

"For all the Saints, who from their labors rest,
Who Thee by faith before the world confessed,
Thy name, O Jesu, be forever bless'd,
    Alleluia.
O may Thy soldiers, faithful, true, and bold,
Fight as the saints who nobly fought of old,
And win, with them, the victor's crown of gold.
    Alleluia.

—*W. W. How.*

HOOKER has these wise and weighty words concerning the observance of Saints' Days: "Forasmuch as we know that Christ hath not only been manifested great in Himself, but great in other His Saints also, the days of whose departure out of the world are to the Church of Christ as the birth and coronation days of kings or emperors, therefore especial choice being made of the very flower of all occasions in this kind, there are annual selected times to meditate of Christ glorified in them who had the honor to suffer for His sake before they had age and ability to know Him [the Holy Innocents]; glorified in them which knowing Him as Stephen, had the sight of that before death whereinto so acceptable death did lead; glorified in those sages of the East that came from far to adore Him and were conducted by strange light; glorified in the second Elias of the world sent before Him to prepare His way; glorified in every

of those Apostles whom it pleased Him to use as founders of His kingdom here; glorified in the Angels as in Michael."[1]

There are two classes of Saints' Days in the English Calendar. The most important commemorate Saints of the New Testament, and, with certain other festivals, are called "red-letter days," because they were usually written or printed in red ink. The less important, commemorating Bishops, Martyrs, and Confessors of a later date and having no special services appointed for them, were called "black-letter days" for a similar reason. At the American revision in 1789, and the Irish in 1870, the black-letter days were all omitted. This in many respects was a distinct loss, inasmuch as most of the days commemorated holy men and women of the British, Irish, Scottish, and English Churches as well as of other branches of the Holy Catholic Church throughout the world, thus witnessing in a very definite way to the historic continuity of the English-speaking Church with the Church of all the ages. For this reason it is much to be desired that the Irish and American Churches should restore or provide commemorations for such notable names as S. Ignatius and S. Polycarp of Asia; S. Cyprian, S. Perpetua, S. Athanasius, and S. Augustine of Africa; S. Agnes, S. Ambrose, S. Jerome, and S. Gregory of Italy; S. Hilary of France; S. David of Wales; S. Patrick, and S. Columba of Ireland; S. Alban, S. Augustine of Canterbury, S. Hugh of Lincoln, and the Venerable Bede of England; and S. Boniface of England and Germany.

It was of Athanasius, "Keen-visioned Seer," the great defender of the Divinity of our Lord in the fourth century, that Newman wrote as an Anglican:

[1] *Ecc. Pol.* V. lxx. 8.

THE SAINTS' DAYS

> "When shall our northern Church her champion see,
> Raised by divine decree,
> To shield the ancient Truth at his own harm?
> Like him who stayed the arm
> Of tyrannous power, and learning sophist-tone,
> Keen-visioned Seer, alone."

And of others:

> "Cyprian is ours, since the high-souled primate laid
> Under the traitorous blade
> His silvered head. And Chrysostom we claim
> In that clear eloquent flame
> And deep-taught zeal in the same woe, which shone
> Bright round a Martyr's throne.
>
> "And Ambrose reared his crosier as of old,
> Less honored, but as bold,
> When in dark times our champion crossed a king."
> —*Lyra Apostolica.*

Among the red-letter days there are only sixteen devoted to the remembrance of New Testament Saints, most of them *Apostles;* one to **S. Stephen;** one to the **Holy Innocents** (in England popularly called **Childermas**); one to **S. Michael and All Angels,** and one to **All Saints. The Annunciation of the Blessed Virgin Mary** (the true feast of the Incarnation), and **The Presentation of Christ in the Temple,** commonly called **The Purification of Saint Mary the Virgin,** may be regarded in a double capacity as the commemorations of her who was declared to be "blessed among women,"[1] and also as festivals of our Lord. There is much lost in the true balance and "proportion of faith"[2] when these festivals are ignored or forgotten.

The day chosen for the commemoration of Saints is

[1] S. Luke i. 28.   [2] Rom. xii. 6.

usually the day of their death, that being their birthday, *dies natalis*, into the higher life of Paradise. But there are two exceptions to this rule, namely, **The Nativity of S. John Baptist,** and **The Conversion of S. Paul.** Of the former S. Augustine wrote, "The Church celebrates two birthdays only, John's and Christ's." Assuming that December 25th and June 24th ("the sixth month"[1] before), are the correct dates, it is curious to note how the days correspond to the two solstices.[2] Even Augustine could see in the dates the fulfilment of the Baptist's own self-effacing confession, "He must increase, but I must decrease,"[3] since the days lengthen from the Nativity of Christ, while they shorten from the Nativity of S. John.

> "How didst thou start, thou holy Baptist, bid
>   To pour repentance on the Sinless Brow!
> Then all thy meekness, from thy hearers hid,
>   Beneath the ascetic's port and preacher's fire,
> Flowed forth, and with a pang thou didst desire
>   He might be chief, not thou."
>
> —*Newman, Lyra Apostolica.*

In this connection also some have seen in the date of S. Thomas's festival (December 21st), when the sun seems to hesitate at the winter solstice, a certain fitness to the doubting character of that Apostle. "S. Andrew's Day," Bishop John Wordsworth says, "is perhaps the only festival of an Apostle claiming to be really on the

---

[1] S. Luke i. 36.

[2] The reason why the 24th was chosen instead of the 25th, which would be exactly six months before Christmas Day, is this: the dates were fixed when the old notation of the days was in use. As December had 31 days and June had only 30, the 8th before the calends of January would be December 25, whereas the 8th before the calends of July would be June 24.

[3] S. John iii. 30.

anniversary of his death."[1] All the more striking therefore is the significance of the date (November 30th) at the beginning of Advent, as S. Andrew was the first of the Twelve Disciples chosen by our Lord, and as he was the first to lead his brother Peter and others to Christ.

The practice of commemorating the lives of Christian saints seems to have originated in the holding of services beside the grave of martyrs on the anniversary of their deaths. We have accounts of these in the martyrdom of Ignatius, Bishop of Antioch (d. A.D. 115), Polycarp, Bishop of Smyrna (d. A.D. 166), and the martyrs of Lyons and Vienne (d. A.D. 177). S. Peter and S. Paul were commemorated very early, and on the same day, June 29th, and it is to be regretted that the English revisers of the Calendar omitted S. Paul on that day, leaving his conversion on January 25th as his only memorial, a feast which dates only from the ninth century.

It is worthy of note that the three holy days following Christmas, December 26th, 27th, and 28th, may have been placed there close to our Lord's Nativity to illustrate the three kinds of martyrdom; S. Stephen nearest as a martyr both in will and deed; S. John next as a martyr in will though not in deed; the Holy Innocents as martyrs in deed though not in will.

"The commemoration of Saints," writes Bishop Westcott, "is one of the provisions that has been wisely made by our Church to bring home to us our connection with the invisible life; to help us to confess that they who once lived to God live still; to know that we are heirs not of a dead past, but of a past fresh with new lessons; to learn that consecrated gifts become an eternal blessing; to understand—most touching mystery—that Christ

[1] *Ministry of Grace*, p. 419.

is pleased to reveal Himself little by little, 'in many parts and in many fashions,' in the persons of His servants. Thus it is that each saint received and shows some trait of the perfect Manhood of His Master. And 'we that are but parts' can recognize in a scale suited to our weakness, now this grace and now that, according to our needs."[1]

"Let us live," writes Bishop Ellicott, "as if they were still with us in the flesh; let us make ourselves meet to enjoy the fulness of communion with them hereafter. Oh, let us bless God for their examples; let us pray to Him for strength to emulate their self-denial, for grace to follow after their meek wisdom, for courage patiently and hopefully to labor in the service of God, even as they labored—to live as they lived, and to die as they died."[2] Or again, as Newman expresses this thought of the great Saints: "They animate us by their example; they cheer us by their company; they are on our right hand and on our left, Martyrs, Confessors, and the like, high and low, who used the same creeds, and celebrated the same mysteries, and preached the same Gospel as we do. And to them were joined, as ages went on, even in fallen times, nay, even now in times of division, fresh and fresh witnesses from the Church below. In the world of spirits there is no difference of parties. . . . Greece and Rome, England and France, give no color to those souls which have been cleansed in the one Baptism, nourished by the One Body, and moulded by the One Faith. . . . Therefore it is good to throw ourselves into the unseen world, it is 'good to be there,' and to build tabernacles for those who speak 'a pure language' and 'serve the Lord with one consent'; not indeed to draw them forth from their

[1] *Social Aspects of Christianity.* [2] *The Destiny of the Creature.*

secure dwelling-places, not superstitiously to honor them, or wilfully to rely on them, lest they be a snare to us, but silently to contemplate them for our edification." [1]

[1] *Parochial and Plain Sermons*, vol. iii.

CHAPTER XV

THE FEAST OF S. MICHAEL AND ALL ANGELS

"Therefore with Angels and Archangels, and with all the company of heaven, we laud and magnify Thy glorious Name; evermore praising Thee and saying, HOLY, HOLY, HOLY, Lord God of Hosts, Heaven and earth are full of Thy glory; Glory be to Thee, O Lord Most High."—*Order for the Holy Communion*.

Two of the most beautiful and most helpful festivals of the year come as "the sere and yellow leaf" begins to remind us of the end of all things, and of our own brief life on earth, namely, the feasts of **S. Michael and All Angels, or Michaelmas, and All Saints.** One tells us of that "innumerable company"[1] "ordained and constituted" by God, not only to "do Him service in heaven," but "that they may succor and defend us on earth".[2] The other speaks of the "great cloud of witnesses"[3] watching and waiting for us in Paradise; "the glorious company of the Apostles, the goodly fellowship of the Prophets, the noble army of Martyrs"; but especially on this day, those "whom we have loved, and lost awhile." Both days are important to recall us from our forgetfulness of "the things which are unseen" and yet alone are "eternal." "Persons," says Newman, "commonly speak as if the other world did not exist now, but would after death. No, it exists now, though we see it not. It is among us and around us. Jacob was shown this in his dream. Angels were all about him though he knew it not. And what Jacob saw in his sleep, that

[1] Heb. xii. 22.   [2] *Collect for All Angels*.   [3] Heb. xii. 1

S. MICHAEL AND ALL ANGELS

Elisha's servant saw as if with his eyes; and the shepherds at the time of the Nativity not only saw but heard."[1]

There are only two angels mentioned by name in the canonical Scriptures, namely Gabriel[2] and Michael.[3] The special commemoration of S. Michael is due doubtless to the fact that he is named in Scripture as a "prince" or "archangel" among the holy inhabitants of heaven. It is a reminder to us that in heaven, as in the Church on earth, there must be many gradations as well as "many mansions." Even there also "all members have not the same office."[4] The angelic host, or "Sabaoth," has its unequal, vastly diverse personal intelligences. "It has its ranks, its degrees, its various celestial nationalities, so to speak. Daniel tells of 'princes' in the heavenly host, and Holy Scripture elsewhere gives us at least nine orders of the celestial hierarchy, angels, archangels, cherubim, seraphim, thrones, dominions, virtues, principalities, powers."[5] In "the books called Apocrypha" two other "princes" among the angels are mentioned by name; Raphael in Tobit viii. 2, and xii. 15, and Uriel in II. Esdras v. 20. The feast of S. Michael the Archangel has been observed in the Eastern Church for 1500 years at least. In the Western Church the day has been September 29th; in the East, November 8th.

Practical Christians of to-day are apt to look upon such a commemoration as a pious sentiment fitted rather for imaginative women or childish men. But plainly

[1] *Parochial and Plain Sermons*, vol. iv.
[2] Dan. viii. 16; ix. 21; S. Luke i. 19, 26.
[3] Dan. x. 13, 21; xii. 1; S. Jude 9; Rev. xii. 7.   [4] Rom. xii. 4.
[5] Col. i. 16; Eph. i. 21; W. Gwynne, *Some Purposes of Paradise*, p. 55.

our Lord did not so judge. In the prayer which He framed for all lips and for our daily use, He deliberately inserted one petition which directs our thought continually to those holy beings, and bids us pray, "Thy will be done on earth as it is done in heaven," that is, by the Angels. As a direct result of His own entrance into this world as Man, there is, He tells us, a great influx, not only of spiritual *power*, but of spiritual *persons*, as helpers in that mighty work which He came to do for men. "Ye shall see heaven open," He said to Nathanael, "and the angels of God ascending and descending upon the Son of Man."[1] What the ladder was to Jacob in his night vision, Christ would have us know, the Son of Man who was also the Son of God is to us, a ladder connecting heaven and earth, a channel for the tender care and ministrations of angels. Before His coming such ministries were but fitful and infrequent. Not until Christ was born, and angels sang their *Gloria in Excelsis* over the fields of Bethlehem, not until they waited on Him in His Temptation, and comforted Him in His Agony, and watched at His Sepulchre, and worshipped Him at His Ascension, was that Way fully opened, and that Ladder set up in all its fulness from earth to heaven. No one can read the later books of the New Testament without seeing that all their writers considered the presence and ministration of angels, not as a devout poetical imagination, but as a sober actual fact in the every-day experience of every Christian. "We are come," exclaims one of these writers, "to an innumerable company of angels."[2] "Are they not all ministering spirits," he asks, "sent forth to minister to them who shall be heirs of salvation?"[3] "Angels came and ministered unto him" is doubtless the simple description of

[1] S. John i. 51.   [2] Heb. xii. 21.   [3] Heb. i. 14.

many an event, an assuaged sorrow or a conquered temptation, in our own lives, as it was in that of our Lord.[1]

The human heart left to its own devices, its sorrows or its struggles, would say "Give me back the spirits of my friends, my loved ones, my children, to be near me and to comfort me." It cries with Tennyson,

> "Be near me when my light is low,
>   When the blood creeps, and the nerves prick
>   And tingle; and the heart is sick,
> And all the wheels of being slow."
>
> —*In Memoriam.*

That is the heart's unreasoning wish. It is the way of fanaticisms in every age, necromancy, and so-called spiritualism, and it is just that which Scripture frowns on and forbids. On the other hand, the promise of angelic messengers in the Bible is full and unreserved. No petition for that loving guardianship is too great for God's fulfilment. Other ages may have been in danger of thinking too much of these heavenly helpers; our danger is that of thinking too little, and therefore slighting and despising them. "He shall give His angels charge over thee to keep thee in all thy ways" is a promise of which we are all too forgetful, and for which All Angels' Day is the wholesome and most necessary reminder. It is of their ministry to us on earth that Edmund Spenser writes:

> "How oft do they their silver bowers leave,
>   To come to succor us that succor want,
>   How oft do they with golden pinions cleave
>   The flitting skies like flying pursuivant,
>   Against foul fiends to aid us militant!

[1] S. Matt. iv. 11.

> They for us fight, they watch and duly ward,
> And their bright squadrons round about us plant;
> And all for love, and nothing for reward—
> O why should heavenly God to men have such regard?"
> —*Fairy Queen*, II. viii. 2.

It is related of Richard Hooker, the great defender of the Church's "polity," that his friend Dr. Saravia, finding him "deep in contemplation" during his last day on earth, asked him concerning his thoughts, to which Hooker replied, "That he was meditating the number and nature of angels, and their blessed obedience and order, without which, peace could not be in heaven; and oh that it might be so on earth."[1]

[1] *Life*, by Isaac Walton.

CHAPTER XVI

THE FEAST OF ALL SAINTS

" 'Tis sweet, as year by year we lose
Friends out of sight, in faith to muse
How grows in Paradise our store."
—*Keble, Burial of the Dead.*

"Give them rest, O Lord, there in the land of the living, in Thy Kingdom, in the delight of Paradise, in the bosom of Abraham, Isaac, and Jacob, our holy fathers, whence pain, sorrow, and groaning is exiled, where the light of Thy countenance looks down and always shines."—*Liturgy of S. James.*

A FESTIVAL in honor of **All Saints** was observed by the Greeks as early as the fourth century on what we call Trinity Sunday. It was not, however, until the middle of the ninth century that the festival became generally observed throughout the West, and then the day chosen was November 1st. The early English name for the day was **All Hallows,** that is, *All Holies*. It is from this we derive the popular name for the preceding day, **Hallowe'en,** or the Even of All Hallows, October 31st.

It is evident that the adoption of this festival was a natural instinct of the human heart and its needs; a day which would not be confined to the remembrance of the *great* Saints and Martyrs of the whole Catholic Church, or of national or local Churches, but of all those devout and unnamed or unknown servants of God who "have departed this life in His faith and fear." The purpose was plainly to give to every individual Christian opportunity to remember their own holy dead as still "living unto God" in Paradise, still members of the One Holy Catholic and Apostolic Church, the Communion of Saints, "no longer trammelled and fettered, compelled to fight for very life in an enemy's country, but free to love, free to will and to obey, free to worship and to work, as they never were in the days of their earthly existence."[1] And not only to remember them, but to pray for their peace and progress that "we, with all those who are departed in the true faith of God's holy Name, may have our perfect consummation and bliss, both in body and soul, in His eternal and everlasting glory" at the Resurrection of the Dead[2] (*Burial Office*).

For such a day in remembrance of the faithful departed, and especially our own, there is and always will be great need. As with the Holy Angels, so with the disembodied spirits of the faithful, there is always great danger of our forgetfulness. They have passed out of sight indeed, but they are not separated from us. "The gates of Hades," or the unseen world of spirits, can "not prevail against" the Church to separate them from it. They are no more beyond our love, or the influence of our prayers than when they were on earth, though doubtless they have less need of them. "The souls of the righteous are in the hand of God, and there shall no torment touch them."[3] They are "in Paradise," but Paradise is not Heaven. "I am not yet ascended," our Lord said to Mary Magdalene on Easter morning, though He had been in Paradise ever since He gave up the

---

[1] *Some Purposes of Paradise*, p. 49.

[2] That prayer of the faithful departed is scriptural, primitive, natural, Christian, see *Some Purposes of Paradise*, Chapters XI and XII.

[3] Wisdom, iii. 1.

THE FEAST OF ALL SAINTS

ghost on the cross on Good Friday.[1] Paradise, Scripture plainly tells us, is only the place of preparation for the Resurrection and for Heaven. To quote some words which I have used elsewhere: "Paradise was the word in common use throughout the East, among Persians and Greeks as well as Hebrews, for a royal park. It was not the king's palace, but the royal garden surrounding the palace, with its cool delights and shady walks; not Heaven, but the ante-chamber of Heaven, where souls might pause a while before the king came out to bring them in to His secret presence-chamber, His supreme delights."[2]

In an age when this truth of the Intermediate State between death and the Resurrection, so plainly revealed in the New Testament, has passed largely out of the thought of multitudes of Christian people, **All Saints' Day** is of more practical importance than ever. Other great days in the Christian Year bring to our remembrance events of a distant past. This recalls us to the immediate present. It is a constant witness and reminder to us of that holy place and that "great multitude which no man can number,"[3] the vast majority indeed of Christ's Holy Church, who are even now advancing in knowledge and grace, and preparing with longing expectation for the fulness of Christ's victory at His second coming.

It is such thoughts as these that All Saints' Day brings home to us, as no other day in the Christian Year can do so fully. To the Christian the death line seems to have vanished. "The death of the body is indeed rarely mentioned in the New Testament, and in no place is it represented either as the end or the beginning

[1] S. John xx. 17.
[2] *Some Purposes of Paradise*, p. 21.   [3] Rev. vii. 9.

of life. To all it is but a stage in life's journey, and not the attainment of its goal. To the Christian it is but the striking of a tent,[1] the 'unloosing' of sails and rudder-bands, as S. Paul twice calls it.[2] It is merely the preparation for another and a sunnier stretch of sea, but one whose true haven is not reached until the Resurrection and the Judgment. It is said even of the elder saints who 'died in faith, not having received the promises,' that ' they *now* [that is, in Paradise] desire a better country, that is, an heavenly . . . for God hath prepared for them a city.' "[3]

> "Sweet is the calm of Paradise the blest.
> But lo! there breaks a yet more glorious day;
> The saints triumphant rise in bright array;
> The King of Glory passes on His way.
> Alleluia."
>
> —*Bishop W. W. How.*

A Day of National Thanksgiving

Thanksgiving Day is peculiar to the American Church in having a special Collect, Epistle, and Gospel provided for it. It is to be "observed as a day of Thanksgiving to Almighty God, for the Fruits of the Earth, and all other Blessings of His merciful Providence" (*Rubric*). The observance probably had its origin in the Harvest Home festivals which were, and are still, common in the English Church. The first settlers in New England seem to have brought the custom with them to America. When the revision of the Prayer Book was adopted by the General Convention in 1789, the date was fixed for "the first Thursday in November, or such other day as shall be appointed by the Civil Authority." The Civil

---

[1] 2 Cor. v. 1. [2] Phil. i. 23; 2 Tim. iv. 6.
[3] Heb. xi. 13, 16. *Some Purposes of Paradise*, pp. 27, 28.

Authority, that is, the Governors of the different States of the Union, and the President of the United States, are now accustomed to appoint the *last* Thursday in that month. The observance, outside the Church, was largely confined to New England and her people until after the Civil War (1861 to 1865), when it became a Day of National Thanksgiving.

CHAPTER XVII

THE BLACK-LETTER DAYS

"Oh live ye by the Calendar,
And with the good ye dwell;
The Spirit that comes down on them
Shall lighten you as well."
—*Coxe, Christian Ballads.*

A Black-Letter Day is a minor festival for which no "liturgical proper," that is, Collect, Epistle, and Gospel, with "Proper Lessons," "Proper Psalms," etc., is provided. The basis of the present Calendar of the Church of England, as finally revised in 1661, is that of the Use of Sarum, both in its Missal, or Service for the Holy Communion, and its Breviàry, or choir offices. Many of the Sarum commemorations, which had grown altogether too numerous, were at this time omitted, and a few names such as the Venerable Bede and S. Alban, which were strangely absent from the Sarum Use, were added. The revision of this part of the Book of Common Prayer, in the matter of the minor festivals, is generally regarded as most unsatisfactory both in what might well have been added and what was omitted.

The reasons which actuated the Bishops at this revision may best be gathered from their answer to the Puritans, who desired the omission of all but four of the black-letter days. They said, "The other names are left in the Calendar, not that they should be so kept as holy days, but they are useful for the preservation of their memories, and for other reasons, as for leases, law-days, etc."

THE BLACK-LETTER DAYS

In the present English Calendar as given below, the red-letter days are printed in heavy type. The notes which I have added in italics are intended to give a few facts in regard to the persons or events commemorated, together with the date of death or of occurrence. A Confessor is one who has suffered persecution for the faith.

January

1. **Circumcision of our Lord.**
6. **Epiphany of our Lord.**
8. Lucian, Priest and Martyr. *Of France*, A.D. 290.
13. Hilary, Bishop and Confessor. *Of Poictiers*, A.D. 368. *This festival gives its name to the Hilary term in the law courts, which begins January 11th and ends January 31st.*
18. Prisca, Roman Virgin and Martyr. A.D. 275.
20. Fabian, Bishop of Rome and Martyr. A.D. 250.
21. Agnes, Roman Virgin and Martyr. A.D. 304.
22. Vincent, Spanish Deacon and Martyr. A.D. 304.
25. **Conversion of S. Paul.**

February

2. **Purification of the Blessed Virgin Mary.**
3. Blasius, an Armenian Bishop and Martyr. A.D. 316.
5. Agatha, a Sicilian Virgin and Martyr. A.D. 251.
14. Valentine, Bishop and Martyr. *Of Rome.* A.D. 270.
24. **S. Matthias, Apostle and Martyr.**

March

1. David, Archbishop of Menevia. *Also named Dewi, national Saint of Wales.* A.D. 544.
2. Cedde, or Chad, Bishop of Lichfield. A.D. 673.

7. Perpetua, Mauritanian Martyr. A.D. 203.
12. Gregory M., Bishop of Rome and Confessor. *M. in this case does not stand for Martyr, but for Magnus, or the Great. It was this Bishop who sent Augustine to England in 596 to convert the Anglo-Saxons. Died* A.D. 604.
18. Edward, King of the West Saxons. A.D. 978.
21. Benedict, Abbot. *Founder of the Benedictine order of Monks, of Mount Cassino, Italy.* A.D. 543.
25. **Annunciation of the Blessed Virgin Mary.**

April

3. Richard, Bishop of Chichester. A.D. 1253.
4. S. Ambrose, Bishop of Milan. A.D. 397.
19. Alphege, Archbishop of Canterbury. *Martyred by the Danes.* A.D. 1012.
23. S. George, Martyr. *Native of Cappadocia, a soldier in the Roman army in the time of Diocletian, early in the fourth century. The Patron Saint of England since* A.D. 1220.
25. **S. Mark, Evangelist and Martyr.**

May

1. **S. Philip and S. James, Apostles and Martyrs.**
3. Invention of the Cross. *Commemorates the Invention that is, the Finding, of the cross on which our Lord suffered, by the Empress Helena, the mother of Constantine, the first Christian Emperor; about* A.D. 326.
6. S. John Evangelist, ante Portam Latinam. *Commemorates his miraculous deliverance when cast into a cauldron of boiling oil "before the Latin Gate" of Rome in the time of Domitian.*

THE BLACK-LETTER DAYS

19. Dunstan, Archbishop of Canterbury. A.D. 988.
26. Augustine, first Archbishop of Canterbury. A.D. 604.
27. Venerable Bede, Priest. *Abbott of Jarrow, the most distinguished scholar of his age, and the first historian of the English Church.* A.D. 735.

June

1. Nicomede, Roman Priest and Martyr. A.D. 90.
5. Boniface, Bishop of Mentz and Martyr. *Called the Apostle of Germany; native of England, and originally named Winfrid.* A.D. 755.
11. **S. Barnabas, Apostle and Martyr.**
17. S. Alban, Martyr. The *first recorded British Martyr*, A.D. 303. *The Sarum Calendar gave the 22d as the day.*
20. Translation of Edward, King of the West Saxons. *Murdered* A.D. 978; *body reinterred* A.D. 981. *See March,* 18th.
24. **Nativity of S. John Baptist.**
29. **S. Peter, Apostle and Martyr.**

July

2. Visitation of the Blessed Virgin Mary. *That is, to her cousin Elizabeth.*[1]
4. Translation of S. Martin, Bishop and Confessor. *Reinterment of his body in a new church dedicated to his honor near Tours, his see city.* A.D. 397. *See Nov.* 11.
15. Swithun, Bishop of Winchester, Translation. *Also spelled Swithin. Celebrated for his humility, as well as his deeds of charity. "He died July 2 A.D. 862, and was buried at his own request outside the*

[1] S. Luke i. 39, etc.

church, where men might walk over him, and the rain water his grave. In A.D. 971 *the relics were translated to a rich shrine within the cathedral; but it is recorded that a most violent rain fell on the destined day, and continued for thirty-nine days, whence arose the popular notion that if it rain on S. Swithin's Day, it will for thirty-nine following.*"[1]

20. Margaret, Virgin and Martyr at Antioch (*in Pisidia*). A.D. 278.
22. S. Mary Magdalen.
25. **S. James, Apostle and Martyr.**
26. S. Anne, Mother of the Blessed Virgin Mary. *Not named in Holy Scripture, but early tradition speaks of her and her husband Joachim as the parents of the Blessed Virgin.*

August

1. Lammas Day. "*The observation of this day as a feast of thanksgiving for the firstfruits of the corn dates from Saxon times, in which it was called Hlaf-maesse, or Loaf-mass, from the offering, at the Mass, of bread made of the new corn. . . . This is one of the four Cross-quarter days, at which rents were formerly due.*"[2]
6. Transfiguration of our Lord. See pp. 62, 63.
7. Name of Jesus. See p. 59.
10. S. Laurence, Archdeacon of Rome and Martyr, A.D. 258.
24. **S. Bartholomew, Apostle and Martyr.**
28. S. Augustine, Bishop of Hippo, Confessor and Doctor. A.D. 430.
29. Beheading of S. John Baptist. *S. Matt.* xiv. 1-13.

[1] Blunt's *Annotated Prayer Book*, p. [51].   [2] Ib., p. [53].

THE BLACK-LETTER DAYS

September

1. Giles, Abbot and Confessor. *Diocese of Nismes, France.* A.D. 725.
7. Eunurchus, Bishop of Orleans. *Also named Evortius.* A.D. 340.
8. Nativity of the Blessed Virgin Mary. *See p. 127.*
14. Holy Cross Day. *Commemorates the public exhibition of the "true cross," which took place on September 14th, A.D. 335, in the church erected in Jerusalem by the Empress Helena in honor of its " invention," or finding. See May 3d.*
17. Lambert, Bishop and Martyr. *Of Maestricht in the Netherlands.* A.D. 709.
21. **S. Matthew, Apostle, Evangelist, and Martyr.**
26. S. Cyprian, Archbishop of Carthage, and Martyr. A.D. 258.
29. **S. Michael and All Angels.**
30. S. Jerome, Priest, Confessor, and Doctor. A.D. 420.

October

1. Remigius, Bishop of Rhemes. *Also called Remi.* A.D. 535.
6. Faith, Virgin, and Martyr. *Of France; Latin name Fides.* A.D. 290.
9. S. Denys Areopagite, Bishop and Martyr. *Abbreviated from Dionysius. Not the Bishop of Paris, who was also a Martyr in A.D. 272, and the patron saint of France; but Dionysius the Areopagite, the first Bishop of Athens, who died A.D. 96. Acts xvii. 34.*
13. Translation of King Edward Confessor. *Died A.D. 1066; the body removed in 1163 to the new shrine in Westminster Abbey (which he had refounded).*

17. Etheldreda, Virgin. *Daughter of the King of the East Angles. Died June 23d, A.D. 679; body translated to new tomb, October 17, A.D. 695.*
18. **S. Luke, Evangelist.**
25. Crispin, Martyr. *In the Salisbury Calendar he was commemorated with his twin brother Crispinian. Shakespeare makes Henry V. exclaim at the battle of Agincourt, "Crispin Crispian shall ne'er go by, . . . But we in it shall be remembered." (IV. sc. iii). The brothers were companions of S. Denys, the first Bishop of Paris, and worked as shoemakers in order to support themselves as missionaries. They were beheaded in A.D. 288, and became the Patron Saints of shoemakers.*
28. **S. Simon and S. Jude, Apostles and Martyrs.**

November

1. **All Saints' Day.**
6. Leonard, Confessor. *Deacon and nobleman of France.* A.D. 599.
11. S. Martin, Bishop and Confessor. *Born in Hungary, military tribune in Constantine's army; became Bishop of Tours in France. Died A.D. 397. "Martinmas" is still one of the four Cross-quarter days in England.*
13. Britius, Bishop. *Also called Brice. Friend and successor of S. Martin as Bishop of Tours.* **Died** A.D. 444.
15. Machutus, Bishop. *Known also as S. Malo.* **Born** *in Wales; became Bishop of Aleth in Brittany.* **Died** A.D. 564.
17. Hugh, Bishop of Lincoln. *Born in Burgundy.* **Died A.D. 1200.**

THE BLACK-LETTER DAYS 99

20. Edmund, King and Martyr. *East Anglia, killed by the Danes*, A.D. 870.
22. Cecilia, Virgin and Martyr. *Of Rome, Patron Saint of music.* A.D. 230.
23. S. Clement I., Bishop of Rome and Martyr. A.D. 100. *See Phil. iv.* 3.
25. Catherine, Virgin and Martyr. A.D. 307, *at Alexandria.*
30. **S. Andrew, Apostle and Martyr.**

December

6. Nicolas, Bishop of Myra in Lycia. A.D. 342.
8. Conception of the Blessed Virgin Mary. *See* pp. 127, 128.
13. Lucy, Virgin and Martyr. *Of Syracuse in Sicily.* A.D. 304.
16. O Sapientia. *This is merely a liturgical note to show that here begin the eight Advent antiphons to the Magnificat, the last coming on December 23d. The first words of the first antiphon are "O Sapientia," or "O Wisdom."*
21. **S. Thomas, Apostle and Martyr.**
25. **Christmas Day.**
26. **S. Stephen, the first Martyr.**
27. **S. John, Apostle and Evangelist.**
28. **Innocents' Day.**
31. Silvester, Bishop of Rome. A.D. 335.

The three following red-letter days were omitted from the Calendar of the Church of England in 1859: January 30th, King Charles the Martyr; May 29th, Charles II., Nativity and Return; November 5th, Papists' Conspiracy.

Much information concerning the black-letter Saints

and Days is to be found in Blunt, *Annotated Prayer Book*, pp. [36] to [61]. Writing of the Calendar as a whole, Mr. Blunt says: "It will be seen that the whole number of individual Saints commemorated is seventy-three. Of these, twenty-one are especially connected with our Blessed Lord; twenty are Martyrs in the age of persecutions; twenty-one are specially connected with our own Church; and eleven are either great and learned defenders of the Faith, like S. Hilary and S. Augustine, or Saints of France, whose names were probably retained as a memorial of the ancient close connection between the Churches of France and England."

Bishop Dowden writes: "It must be confessed that the black-letter saints of the modern English Calendar form by no means an ideal presentation of the worthies and heroes of the Church Catholic. The Bishop of Salisbury [J. Wordsworth] has some admirable remarks on the future reform of our English Calendar in his *Ministry of Grace*, pp. 421-425."[1]

"O God of Saints, to Thee we cry;
O Saviour, plead for us on high;
O Holy Ghost, our Guide and Friend,
Grant us Thy grace till life shall end;
That with all Saints our rest may be
In that bright Paradise with Thee."
—*Bishop Maclagan.*

[1] *The Church Year*, p. 152.

CHAPTER XVIII

THE FASTS OF THE CHRISTIAN YEAR

> " 'Lord, I have fasted, I have prayed,
>   And sackcloth has my girdle been,
>   To purge my soul I have assayed
>   With hunger blank and vigil keen.
>   O God of mercy! why am I
>   Still haunted by the self I fly? '
>
> "Sackcloth is a girdle good,
>   O bind it round thee still;
>   Fasting, it is Angels' food,
>   And Jesus loved the night air chill;
>   Yet think not prayer and fast were given
>   To make one step 'twixt earth and heaven."
>   —*R. Hurrell Froude, Lyra Apostolica.*

FASTS equally with feasts are particularly open to abuse. Christians as well as ancient Jews can keep fast in such a way as to cause men merely to ridicule the custom. One reads to-day of "Lenten outings," "Lenten excursions," and "Lenten entertainments," where the thin disguise of religion is scarcely intended to hide the worldliness. And yet, no matter how much the practice may be perverted or ridiculed, the duty of keeping fast must remain as long as Christ's words remain. As George Herbert puts it:

> "Neither ought other men's abuse of Lent
>   Spoil the good use; lest by that argument
>   We forfeit all our creed."

When the ancient Jews made not only their fasts, but also their feasts, and sacrifices, and prayers "an abomination" in God's sight, He did not abrogate one or other. He merely set His erring people right by telling them what *kind* of feast and fast and prayer was alone acceptable to Him.[1]

And when we come to the teaching of our Lord and His Apostles, we find no different rule. The New Testament as well as the Old is full of directions as to fasting. The caricature and abuse of fasting in our Lord's day may seem to flippant and shallow Christians a convenient excuse for ridiculing and rejecting the whole idea of asceticism as a necessary part of the Christian life. Yet it cannot be too distinctly remembered that it was in face of the most utter abuse of fasting that the Lord Jesus insisted upon the duty as strongly as any Jewish prophet or rabbi ever did. In fact His own ministry begins with a fast, and that, the most rigorous that was ever kept by mortal man. So, too, in His teaching of the multitude in the Sermon on the Mount, intended, we know, as the foundation law of His coming Church, we find Him placing bodily abstinence on the same high level as prayer and almsgiving, not commanding them as duties, but assuming them as already such, and only laying down rules as to how to practise them. He does not say "Ye *shall* fast," but "*When* ye fast," and then, after laying down rules for the observance of the duty, He adds the assurance of His Father's most certain reward for all true and faithful fasting.[2]

On another occasion our Lord defends His disciples for their present omission of fasting, not by declaring the uselessness of the practice, as a thing affecting only the body, but by telling His critics that it was simply

[1] Is. i. 11-16; lviii. 1-8.   [2] S. Matt. vi. 16, 17, 18.

a question of proper times and seasons. The time of His disciples had not yet come. "The Bridegroom," as He calls Himself, was still with them. But the day would come when the Bridegroom would be taken away from them, and "then shall they fast."[1]

When, therefore, their Lord had ascended into heaven, we find great Apostles and humble believers alike practising that which our Lord practised. It was while the Church in Antioch was keeping some penitential season, "as they ministered to the Lord and fasted," that the message came to them by the Holy Ghost to ordain and send out Barnabas and Paul on their great mission.[2] It was to laymen in the Church of Corinth S. Paul, a few years later, gave the special advice that they should "give themselves to fasting and prayer."[3] S. Paul began his own life as a Christian layman with a three-days' fast;[4] in ordaining clergy as an Apostle, it is done by him with "prayer and fasting";[5] and he declares it to be one of the signs of his own faithfulness as a minister of Christ that he had "approved himself in fastings" as well as "in patience and in afflictions."[6]

It is plain then that the religion that drops fasts and fasting out of the list of its duties, or rather from the list of its spiritual "armor,"[7] is not, and cannot be, the religion of Jesus Christ, or of His Apostles, or of His Scriptures. It is "the Scriptures," George Herbert reminds us, that "bid us fast." All that the Church does in Lent and other times is to add the word "now" to our Lord's word "when." Just as she does for His other precepts concerning prayer and almsgiving, so here,

[1] S. Matt. ix. 15. [2] Acts xiii. 1, 2, 3.
[3] 1 Cor. vii. 5. [4] Acts ix. 9.
[5] Acts xiv. 23. [6] 2 Cor. vi. 5; also xi. 27.
[7] Eph. vi. 13.

she simply appoints the times and seasons when they may be most wisely exercised.

But though the authority for fasting is so unquestionable, and its claim upon our obedience so plain, the purpose of it all must be kept distinctly in view if we are to escape grievous errors in regard to it. This purpose is not to be found in any theory that the pain of His creatures is pleasing to God. As a wholesome preparation for the Baptism of adults,[1] and for the Holy Communion, it is primarily an act of reverence in approaching more worthily those holy sacraments. Its chief purpose, however, is for deepening the sense of sin within us, and as an instrument of self-discipline. "The sacrifices of God are a broken spirit,"[2] and we cannot conceive of a truly repentant or broken spirit in one who is perpetually engrossed in the pleasures of the world and the flesh. Christ came to save the body as well as the soul, and that He may do so the body must be brought into subjection to the higher nature. What, therefore, the gymnasium is to the athlete, what the severity of the study is to the scholar, and the drill of camp life is to the soldier, the discipline of fasting and abstinence is to the Christian. The real Lent, writes Bishop Phillips Brooks, "is the putting forth of a man's hand to quiet his own passions and to push them aside, that the higher voices may speak to him and the higher touches fall upon him; it is the making of an emptiness about the soul that the higher fulness may fill it."

It is the peculiarity of our branch of the Church that, while she appoints days and seasons for fasting, she leaves her children free as to the method of their fast. Only two days in the whole year, namely Ash Wednesday and Good Friday, does she name as absolute fasts, when,

[1] See first rubric in service. [2] Ps. li. 17.

so far as our health allows, she expects us to abstain from food until the afternoon, "the ninth hour" (three o'clock) according to the ancient custom. All other days the Church speaks of as "days on which she requires such a measure of abstinence as is more especially suited to extraordinary acts and exercises of devotion."[1] This "measure of abstinence" she does not define. It does not necessarily consist in the substitution of one kind of food for another, but rather in the voluntary giving up for a time of luxuries and pleasures, not only in food and clothing, but also in amusements and entertainments. The final purpose of all such efforts at self-discipline is not to narrow our lives or diminish our joys, for He "giveth us richly all things to enjoy,"[2] but the very opposite. It is to secure for our higher nature a freedom to develop its powers which the world and the flesh are ever tending to contract and cramp. As Wordsworth says:

> "The world is too much with us; late and soon,
> Getting and spending, we lay waste our powers."

[1] "Table of Fasts."   [2] 1 Tim. vi. 17.

CHAPTER XIX

LENT AND PRE-LENT

"Welcome, dear feast of Lent: who loves not thee,
  He loves not temperance, or authority,
    But is composed of passion.
  The Scriptures bid us fast; the Church says, now:
  Give to thy mother what thou wouldst allow
    To every corporation.
.   .   .   .   .

" 'Tis true, we cannot reach Christ's fortieth day;
  Yet to go part of that religious way
    Is better than to rest:
  We cannot reach our Saviour's purity;
  Yet we are bid, 'Be holy e'en as He.'
    In both let's do our best.

"Who goeth in the way which Christ hath gone,
  Is much more sure to meet with Him, than one
    That travelleth by-ways.
  Perhaps my God, though He be far before,
  May turn, and take me by the hand, and more
    May strengthen my decays."
            —*George Herbert, The Temple.*

THE word **Lent** is derived from the Anglo-Saxon *Lencten*, which means Spring. The Latin name is *Quadragesima*, which signifies *fortieth*, in reference to the number of fast days in the season, omitting the six Sundays, which are always feasts. The word Quadragesima is also used once in the Prayer Book for the First Sunday in Lent.[1] *Carême*, the modern French word for Lent, in old French *Quaresme*, is simply an abbreviation and corruption of Quadragesima.

[1] See "Rules for Movable Feasts."

We have here doubtless the origin of the names given to the three Pre-Lenten Sundays which act as a kind of warning of the approaching fast. As the first Sunday in Lent is **Quadragesima** or the fortieth day before Easter, so, in round numbers, **Quinquagesima** is fiftieth, **Sexagesima** sixtieth, and **Septuagesima** seventieth. It is worthy of note in this connection that in the services for all these three Sundays before Lent the Apostle S. Paul is held up as a noble example of zeal, and self-denial, and suffering for Christ. On *Quinquagesima* his great words about the worthlessness of all such self-sacrifice and zeal without love give the true Christian watchword for a right Lent-keeping.

The custom of keeping a fast in preparation for Easter is of very early origin. It is mentioned by Irenæus, the Bishop of Lyons who died in A.D. 202, and by Tertullian, a priest and a native of Carthage, who died in 220. There was at first, however, great variation in the length of the season. Irenæus speaks of it variously as one day, or forty hours, or two days or more. Socrates, the Church historian, who was born in 380, speaks of the fast as three weeks, while Sozomen, who continued Socrates' history down to 440, refers to it as six weeks. "The observance of the forty days of Lent is first distinctly mentioned in the fifth canon of Nicæa, A.D. 325."[1] It was not, however, till the end of the sixth century that the present arrangement of the forty days was established. It was Gregory the Great, the Bishop of Rome who sent Augustine the monk to England in 596, who fixed the beginning of the season on Ash-Wednesday, forty-six days before Easter, thus giving forty days of abstinence by leaving out the Sundays, which are called "in" and not "of" Lent.

[1] Duchesne, p. 365.

"The primary object of the institution of a fast before Easter," writes Mr. Blunt, "was doubtless that of perpetuating in the hearts of every generation of Christians the sorrow and mourning which the Apostles and Disciples felt during the time that the Bridegroom was taken away from them.[1] This sorrow had, indeed, been turned into joy by the Resurrection, but no Easter joys could ever erase from the mind of the Church the memory of those awful forty hours of blank and desolation which followed the last sufferings of her Lord; and she lives over year by year the time from the morning of [the first] Good Friday to the morning of [the first] Easter-Day by a re-presentation of Christ 'evidently set forth crucified among us'.[2] This probably was the earliest idea of a fast before Easter. But it almost necessarily followed that sorrow concerning the death of Christ should be accompanied by sorrow concerning the cause of that death; and hence the Lenten fast became a period of self-discipline; and was so probably from its first institution in Apostolic times. And, according to the literal habit which the early Church had of looking up to the pattern of her Divine Master, the forty days of His fasting in the wilderness, while He was undergoing temptation, became the gauge of the servants' Lent, deriving still more force as an example from the typical prophecy of it which was so evident in the case of Moses and Elijah."[3]

The popular name of **Ash-Wednesday,** the first day of Lent, has been acquired "from the custom of blessing ashes made from the palms distributed on the Palm Sunday of the preceding year, and signing the cross with them on the heads of those who knelt before the officia-

[1] S. Matt. ix. 15.   [2] Gal. iii. 1.
[3] Deut. x. 10; 1 Kings xix. 9. *The Annotated Prayer Book*, p. 90.

ting minister for the purpose, while he said, 'Remember, man, that thou art dust, and unto dust shalt thou return'."[1] The day before Ash-Wednesday is popularly known as **Shrove Tuesday** because, in mediæval days penitents were accustomed to go to private confession on that day, and to be *shriven*, that is, absolved, in preparation for a good Lent. In Shakespeare's time it had become the equivalent of the Italian *carnival*, which signifies "farewell to flesh," in reference to the giving up of flesh-meat during Lent; both words thus acquiring a meaning the reverse of their original one.

Though the Sundays in Lent are not fast days, it may be best to note here the popular name given to the Fourth Sunday. Besides being known as **Mid-Lent Sunday** (in French, *Mi-Carême*), it is commonly called **Refreshment Sunday** on account of the Gospel for the day, which contains the story of the Miraculous Feeding of the Five Thousand in the wilderness.

[1] *Ann. Pr. Bk.*, p. 91.

CHAPTER XX

HOLY WEEK

"We are drawing nearer and nearer to the Cross; and do not our hearts burn within us in the way? To those who really know the love of Christ, which passeth knowledge, what a season is this!"—*Bp. Coxe, Thoughts on the Services.*

> "The royal banners forward go,
> The Cross shines forth in mystic glow,
> Where He in flesh, our flesh who made,
> Our sentence bore, our ransom paid."
> —*V. Fortunatus.*

It is a common mistake to speak of the last week in Lent as **Passion Week.** That name belongs properly to the week preceding. The Fifth Sunday is **Passion Sunday,** when the Epistle for the day begins to tell the story of the great Sacrifice. The correct name for the last week is **Holy Week.** The Germans give it the significant name of *Still,* or *Silent Week.* The Orientals call it the *Great Week.* The first day of the week, the Sixth Sunday or the Sunday next before Easter, is popularly known as **Palm Sunday,** that being the day of our Lord's solemn entry into Jerusalem proclaiming His Messiahship.[1] In "The Pilgrimage of Silvia" she gives us an account of the ceremonies of Holy week in Jerusalem in the fourth century, and of the procession of palm-bearers on Palm Sunday.[2]

As denoting the vast importance of these last days of

---

[1] S. John xii. 13.   [2] Duchesne, p. 484.

HOLY WEEK

our Lord's brief life on earth, it is very significant that more than one-fourth of the four gospels is taken up with the record of the events of Holy Week, beginning with Palm Sunday. Though no attempt is made in the Prayer Book to follow chronologically the scenes leading to and around the Cross which form the one absorbing subject of the Gospels for every day, nevertheless it is well for us to take due note of the events of the three days following Palm Sunday.

On *Monday*, on His way to Jerusalem, our Lord pronounces His judgment on the barren fig-tree as a type of the Jewish Church. He cleanses the Temple for the second time, driving the buyers and sellers from its courts. The chief priests and scribes take counsel to put Him to death.[1]

On *Tuesday* Christ teaches in the Temple; answers the questions of His enemies; speaks many parables; denounces woe on the scribes and Pharisees; sits with His disciples on the Mount of Olives overlooking the city, and foretells its destruction.[2] The last day of His public ministry.

On *Wednesday* He foretells His betrayal. The chief priests agree with Judas for thirty pieces of silver.[3]

Maundy Thursday is the popular name given to the Thursday before Easter, the day on which our Lord made preparation to eat the Passover with His disciples. It was on the evening of this day according to our reckoning, but on the commencement of Good Friday according to the Jewish reckoning, that He ate the Passover, and afterwards instituted the Holy Eucharist at the table, and out of the very elements of the ancient feast, which was but the shadow of the new and infinitely

[1] S. Mark xi. 12–20.
[2] S. Mark xi. 20–end; xii., xiii.   [3] S. Luke xxii. 1–7.

greater feast. Here were given the "new commandments" to "do this in remembrance" of Him, and to "love one another" as He had loved them, and it is from one or other of these "commandments" or "*mandates*" that the day receives its name of *Maundy Thursday*, or *Dies Mandati*.

In mediæval times the particular mandate of our Lord was taken to be the symbolical washing of one another's feet in token of love and humility, for which He had Himself just given them an example.[1] In England two clergy of the highest rank present washed the feet of all in the choir, and of each other. This custom, which is still retained in some portions of the Church, was continued in England by the Sovereigns until the latter part of the seventeenth century (James II was the last to perform the office), and by the Archbishops of York on their behalf until the middle of the eighteenth century.[2]

In the ancient offices of the English Church the commemoration of the Institution of the Holy Eucharist was observed on this day (called *Natalis Calicis*, or the Birthday of the Cup), by a celebration of the Holy Communion at Vespers.[3] This was the custom of the Church in Carthage as early as the year 397, when, "in view of the original institution of the Eucharist having been 'after supper,' it made an express synodical declaration that the rule of fasting communion was binding 'excepto uno die anniversario, quo cœna Domini celebratur,'" that is, except on this single anniversary.[4] S. Augustine in the same century agrees with this view "that it is lawful for the Body and Blood of the Lord to be offered and received after other food has been par-

[1] S. John xiii. 14.   [2] See Blunt, *Ann. Pr. Bk.*, pp. 98, 99.
[3] Blunt, p. 99.
[4] Bingham, *Antiq.*, XXI., c. i. 30; Dowden, p. 41.

taken of, on one fixed day of the year, the day on which the Lord instituted the Supper, in order to give special solemnity to the service on that anniversary." He adds, however, "I think that, in this case, it would be more seemly to have it celebrated at such an hour as would leave it in the power of any who have fasted to attend the service before the repast which is customary at the ninth hour. Wherefore we neither compel, nor do we dare to forbid, any one to break his fast before the Lord's Supper on that day."[1]

In this connection Bishop Coxe has a very thoughtful remark. "Two Thursdays," he writes, "aid us in gaining the full idea of the Eucharist, Maundy Thursday, and 'Holy Thursday,' or Ascension Day. On the first, the bread and wine were taken and received as Christ's Body and Blood, while the unchanged Christ stood before them. On the second, the Body of our Lord became invisible to human eyes; but it is required of faith to behold that Body at the right hand of the Father, and at the same time to 'discern the Lord's Body' in the Lord's Supper. And this is just what the Lord prepared us for[2] when He said, 'Doth this offend you? what and if ye shall see the Son of Man ascend up where He was before?'"

[1] *Ep.* LIV *to Januarius*, c. vii. 9.   [2] S. John vi. 62.

CHAPTER XXI

GOOD FRIDAY AND EASTER-EVEN

"Is it not strange, the darkest hour
   That ever dawned on sinful earth
Should touch the heart with softer power
   For comfort, than an angel's mirth?
That to the Cross the mourner's eye should turn
Sooner than where the stars of Christmas burn?

"Sooner than where the Easter sun
   Shines glorious on yon open grave,
And to and fro the tidings run,
   'Who died to heal, is risen to save'?
Sooner than where upon the Saviour's friends
The very Comforter in light and love descends?"
—*Keble, Christian Year*.

IT would seem as if this thought of Mr. Keble concerning **Good Friday** was the first thought in the mind and heart of the Church in her earliest days. For "strange" indeed as it may appear, the anniversary of our Lord's great Sacrifice upon the Cross was kept at first, not as a fast day, but as a feast. It is in fact strictly speaking of the events of Good Friday, and not of Easter, that S. Paul is thinking when he writes: "Christ our Passover is *sacrificed* for us, therefore let us *keep the feast*."[1] Foreign as it may seem to our thought to-day, Christians, whose whole early life had been spent as Jews in the atmosphere of the Temple, and the Old Testament

[1] 1 Cor. v. 7; "keep festival," R. V. margin.

would naturally think of the anniversary of their Lord's Crucifixion on the great fourteenth day of the month Nisan, as the fulfilment and the successor of their ancient Pascha or Passover, the glorious festal day on which the true Lamb of God offered Himself for their redemption. They would not, and could not, indeed, separate this awful yet most blessed event from that which followed as its necessary complement on Easter Day. For, unlike the lamb of the typical sacrifice, which had no resurrection, their Lord had risen from the dead, and had thus proved Himself to be "the Son of God with power."[1]

It is this double thought also which forms the theme of the old Latin hymn for Easter:

> "At the Lamb's high feast we sing
> Praise to our victorious King,
> Who hath washed us in the tide
> Flowing from His pierced side;
> Praise we Him whose love divine
> Gives His sacred blood for wine,
> Gives His body for the feast,
> Christ the Victim, Christ the Priest."

In endeavoring to account for this fact of Good Friday as at the first a feast day, Bishop Dowden says: "We must suppose that the realization of the blessings of the redemption purchased by the Saviour's blood *overtoned* (to borrow a term from the art of music) the imaginative presentment of the historical sufferings of the Cross. Our own English term, 'Good Friday,'" he adds, "seems to have originated with a similar way of regarding the facts."[2] This method of celebrating the Pascha, or Passover, that is, the day of the Crucifixion, in close union with the two following days, as one feast, lingered on in the

[1] Rom. i. 4.   [2] *The Church Year*, pp. 106, 107.

Church until the Council of Nice in 325. Even at this date we find the Emperor Constantine, in a letter addressed to the Church, stating that the Lord has left us "only one *festal* day of our deliverance, that is to say, of *His holy Passion*." From which it is plain that "the dominant thought connected with the word Pascha was still that of the Crucifixion."[1]

It was not until the Council of Nice that it was definitely settled that the anniversary of the Resurrection should always be held on the Sunday after the day of the Crucifixion, and not on a week-day. Consequently, when this division of the commemoration was made, it was most natural that the previous Friday should acquire much of its present character as a day of profound meditation on our Lord's sufferings, and as a penitential preparation for the joy of Easter.

It is evident from this primitive custom of regarding the Day of the Crucifixion, in conjunction with the two following days, as a festival, that the Holy Eucharist would of course be celebrated on that day. When, however, the separation of the days took place, it was natural that the day of the Crucifixion should be observed in a different way. It is about this time we find the custom of omitting the Consecration growing up in the Church, on the ground of its being inconsistent with the sad memories of that day.[2] This did not, however, prevent the *receiving* of the Holy Communion on Good Friday, as the Sacrament was reserved from the celebration on Maundy Thursday, according to a canon of the Church of England in the tenth century, for the priest, "and whosoever else pleases."[3] "In fact, Martene

[1] Dowden, p. 119.
[2] See Scudamore, *Not. Euch.*, Chapter XVII, sec. 3.
[3] Johnson, *Canons*, i. 404.

proves that Communion of the laity as well as of the priest on this day was the prevailing custom of the Church until the tenth century at least, and there are strong grounds for believing that the practice continued down to the time of the Reformation."[1]

"The appointment of an Epistle and Gospel," Mr. Blunt adds, "is a *prima facie* evidence that Consecration on Good Friday was intended to supersede the Mass of the Pre-sanctified [the reserved Sacrament] which had been hitherto used, and Communion was of course intended to follow. . . . The practice of the Church of England since the Reformation certainly seems to have been to celebrate the Holy Communion on this day. . . . The conclusions that may be drawn are, (1) that the Church of England never intended so far to depart from ancient habits as to be without the Sacramental Presence of Christ on the Day when His Sacrifice is more vividly brought to mind than on any other day of the year; (2) that from the introduction of the un-Catholic custom of Communion by the priest alone, or for some other reason, it was thought best to disuse the Mass of the Pre-sanctified and substitute Consecration; (3) that it is a less evil to depart from ancient usage by consecrating on this day than to be without the Sacramental Presence of our Lord."[2]

It is worthy of note that Bishop King had an early celebration during Holy Week, Good Friday not excepted (1889), in his Cathedral of Lincoln, and that this was also the custom in S. Paul's, London, under Dean Church, Canon Gregory (afterwards Dean), and Dr. Liddon.[3]

It should be observed that **Easter Even** is not an Eve in the usual sense of that word. The term applies to

[1] Blunt, *Ann. Pr. Bk.*, p. 101.
[2] Ib., pp. 101–2.   [3] See Liddon's *Life*, by Johnston, pp. 331–2.

the whole day during which our Lord's Body lay in the sepulchre. Though the Disciples did not yet know it, the battle was fought, and the victory already won, for while the sacred Body rests peacefully in the tomb in Joseph's fragrant garden, in the sunshine, or under the full beams of the Paschal moon, His soul, as the Epistle reminds us, is "preaching," that is, telling the glad tidings of His victory to the departed in Paradise. It is only His friends on earth who see Him not who are sad, because "the Bridegroom is taken away from them."[1]

"At length the worst is o'er, and Thou art laid
  Deep in Thy darksome bed;
All still and cold beneath yon dreary stone
  Thy sacred form is gone;
Around those sacred lips where power and mercy hung,
  The dews of death have clung;
The dull earth o'er Thee, and Thy foes around,
Thou sleep'st a silent corse, in funeral fetters wound.

"Sleep'st Thou indeed? or is Thy spirit fled
  At large among the dead?
Whether in Eden bowers Thy welcome voice
  Wake Abraham to rejoice,
Or in some drearier scene Thine eye controls
  The thronging band of souls;
That, as Thy blood won earth, Thine agony
Might set the shadowy realm from sin and sorrow free."
          —*Keble, Christian Year.*

The Collect with its reference to the fact of our being "buried with Christ in Baptism,"[2] recalls to us the custom of the primitive Church to receive on this day, and early on Easter morning, those catechumens who have been preparing for Holy Baptism during Lent.

"The holy women," writes Bishop Coxe, "have pre-

[1] S. Matt. ix. 15.   [2] Col. ii. 12.

pared their spices, and are unconsciously giving a new meaning to the language of the Canticles: 'I charge you, O ye daughters of Jerusalem, that ye stir not up, nor awake my love, till He please. . . . I will get me to the mountain of myrrh, and the hill of frankincense, until the day break, and the shadows flee away.' "[1]

[1] Song of Solomon, ii. 7; iv. 6; *Thoughts on the Services*, Easter Even.

CHAPTER XXII

"OTHER DAYS OF FASTING"

"Its wisdom is forever old and perpetually new; its calendar celebrates all seasons of the rolling year; its narrative is the simplest, the most pathetic, the most rapturous, and the most ennobling the world has ever known."—*Edmund C. Stedman on The Book of Common Prayer*.

THE other fasts of the Church are:

1. "**The Ember Days** at the Four Seasons, being the Wednesday, Friday, and Saturday after the First Sunday in Lent, the Feast of Pentecost, September 14th, and December 13th. The last two seasons are placed just before the autumnal equinox, and the winter solstice. The word *Ember* is an abbreviation of the German *Quatember*, which in its turn is a corruption of the Latin *Quatuor Tempora*, or Four Seasons. Similarly the French name is *Quatre Temps*.[1]

The Ember Days are the times set apart for special intercession in preparation for the ordination of the Clergy. They have their primary authority in the example of our Lord, whose fast in the Wilderness was the preparation for His own entrance on the Ministry to which, at His Baptism, He had just been "called of God

---

[1] The word, however, may have a double origin in English. According to Professor Skeat its primary root is the Anglo-Saxon "ymbren" from "ymb," round, and "ren," to run, and so equivalent to "circuit," that is, the circuit of the four seasons of the year.—*Etymological Dictionary*, p. 188.

as was Aaron."[1] Before He ordained His Apostles also, He passed the whole night in prayer.[2] Compare the example of the Apostles themselves in Acts xiii. 2, 3; xiv. 23. "He who faithfully keeps the Ember Seasons," writes Bishop Coxe, "will have done more for the Church in his lifetime than a thousand satirists of the Clergy, or an army of censorious declaimers setting forth their own ideas of what the ministry should be. Indeed he has no right to find fault with his spiritual pastors, who has never helped them with the offices which the Church, knowing their peculiar dangers, has provided and enjoined for their assistance and support. How often does the Apostle Paul crave the like benefit from those to whom he ministered! And surely the 'earthen vessels' which bear the treasure of the Gospel now are as much in need of the prayers of the faithful as he was."[3]

2. **The Rogation Days** are "the Monday, Tuesday, and Wednesday before Holy Thursday or the Ascension of our Lord" (Table of Fasts). Rogation means *Asking*, with special reference to the time of His withdrawal from the sight of His Disciples. The Fifth Sunday after Easter, which is the first day of Rogation Week, is usually called *Rogation Sunday*. The Epistle and Gospel for the day have been in use since the fourth century. The fast was probably instituted as early as the fifth century for the purpose of asking God's blessing on the rising produce of the fields. With this view the Irish and American Prayer Books have provided prayers for "Fruitful Seasons" on these days. Mamertus, the Bishop of Vienne in France, is said to have instituted the fast in A.D. 452, when storms and pestilence, coupled with the ravages of the barbarians then threatening

[1] S. Matt. iii. 13 to end; Heb. v. 4, 5.
[2] S. Luke vi. 12, 13.   [3] *Thoughts on the Services.*

the very existence of the Church, had laid waste his diocese and city. As a part of the observances solemn processions with litanies were made in deprecation of God's chastisement.

In view of this origin, the petitions in our own Litany for "the kindly fruits of the earth," against "plague, pestilence, and famine," against "battle and murder, and sudden [that is, violent] death," acquire a profound meaning. With this thought in mind, how impressive too is the appeal, "O God, we have heard with our ears, and our fathers have declared unto us, the noble works that Thou didst in their days and in the old time before them," with its response, "O Lord, arise, help us, and deliver us for Thine honor." And again, "From our enemies defend us, O Christ," with the response, "Graciously look upon our afflictions": "With pity behold the sorrows of our hearts," and its answer, "Mercifully forgive the sins of Thy people." George Herbert tells us in his "Country Parson" that the use of the Litany in procession, with priest and people, around the bounds of the parish, with prayer for a blessing on the fruits of the field, was a custom in his day, and it is still practised in some of the rural parishes of England.

3. **"All the Fridays in the Year"** are fast days, the Church tells us in her Prayer Book, though the great majority of her children seem wholly to forget it. Just as every Sunday is a little Easter, so every Friday should be a little Good-Friday, reminding us continually of the sufferings of our Lord for our redemption. It should at least be a day of quietness, and abstinence from the more exciting pleasures of life. The Fridays have been regarded as fast days from the very earliest times. There is but one exception noted in our Prayer Book, namely, Christmas Day, which is always a feast.

4. Other days of fasting or abstinence appointed by the English Church are the **Vigils** or **Eves** of certain festivals, namely, The Nativity of our Lord, The Purification, The Annunciation, Easter-Day, Ascension-Day, Pentecost, S. Matthias, S. John Baptist, S. Peter, S. James, S. Bartholomew, S. Matthew, S. Simon and S. Jude, S. Andrew, S. Thomas, and All Saints. And the rule is added, "That if any of these Feast-days fall upon a Monday, then the Vigil or Fast-day shall be kept upon the Saturday, and not upon the Sunday next before it." The American Church omitted these vigils in the revision of 1789. The Irish Church retained them in its revision of 1870.

CHAPTER XXIII

VARIATIONS AND REVISIONS OF NATIONAL CALENDARS

"Every scribe which is instructed unto the Kingdom of Heaven is like unto a man that is an householder, which bringeth forth out of his treasure things new and old.—*S. Matt.* xiii. 52.

FROM the earliest age no national branch of the Holy Catholic Church has been without its own Liturgy or Liturgies, that is, an office for the celebration of the Holy Communion. Every Liturgy had also its own Calendar. Dr. John Mason Neale in his English version of the five Primitive Liturgies [1] gives a list of no less than eighty extant national or diocesan variations of these five principal families. Dr. Littledale, who edited the second edition of Dr. Neale's book, gives excerpts from twenty-four other Liturgies "either unknown to Dr. Neale, or beyond his reach at the time when the first edition of his book was published."

All of these hundred and more extant liturgies, in many tongues and of many lands, from India in the East to Spain and Ireland in the West, have certain clearly defined features, such as, among others, (1) the Preparation or Pro-anaphora, down to the *Sursum Corda;* (2) Epistles and Gospels; (3) the Creed; (4) the Offertory; (5) the great Eucharistic Prayer, including the Ter-Sanctus, or Triumphal Hymn, "Holy, Holy, Holy,"

[1] *Translations of the Principal Liturgies.* 1, Of S. James, or Jerusalem; 2, of S. Mark, or Alexandria; 3, of S. Thaddeus, or the East; 4, of S. Peter, or Rome; 5, of S. John, or Ephesus.

VARIATIONS OF NATIONAL CALENDARS 125

the words of Institution, the Oblation, the Invocation of the Holy Ghost (omitted in the Roman); (6) the great Intercession, including the Lord's Prayer; (7) the Prayer of Humble Access, Confession, Communion, and Thanksgiving.

But along with these features which they have in common, there are as many variations in detail as there are "Uses," that is, liturgical forms of the particular country or diocese. Moreover, these various "Uses" have always been subject to revision from age to age according to the special or supposed needs of the time or country. For instance, the Roman Liturgy, which was originally in Greek, and confined to use in the local Greek-speaking Church of Rome, was at some unknown date turned into Latin, which had then become the vernacular of the majority of the Roman Christians. This was revised by Pope Leo I. (440–461); by Pope Gelasius (492–496); by Gregory I. (590–604), and has had many additions made to it in later times. The original Liturgy of the ancient British, Irish, and Scottish Churches had its source in the Ephesine and the Gallican or French Liturgy, but when Augustine came to Canterbury from Rome in 596, he brought the revised Roman service. After these Celtic Churches of the north and west had united with the Italian missions among the Angles and Saxons in the south, a new revision came gradually into use which incorporated many features of the older Churches. After the Norman Conquest Bishop Osmund of Sarum or Salisbury (1078–1099) undertook a new revision of the English service books, and his work was considered so favorably that the "*Missal according to the Use of Sarum*" became practically the Liturgy of the whole English Church, though various other diocesan Uses, such as Hereford, York, Bangor, and Lincoln, and even of S. Paul's Cathedral, London, continued to be employed more or less in the worship of the Church.[1] "It was adopted also in Ireland in the twelfth century, and in various Scottish dioceses in the twelfth and thirteenth centuries."[2]

The next revision of the English Liturgy was that in the sixteenth and seventeenth centuries (1549, 1552, 1561, 1604, 1661), when, as in Rome in the early days, the services were restored to "the tongue understanded of] the people,"[3] and other corrections in practice and doctrine were made.

Together with all these various forms of the Liturgy by nations and dioceses, there were also many and various forms of the Calendar, or order for observing the fasts and festivals of the Christian Year. Here, too, while all branches of the Catholic Church the world over observed the same great outlines of the year based upon the Incarnation, Death, Resurrection, and Ascension of our Lord, and the Coming of the Holy Ghost, each national Church, and often each diocese, had its own particular Use. Originally every Bishop, subject to certain limitations, had power to regulate the Calendar as well as the services of his own diocese. This naturally led to great diversity and multiplicity of festivals, especially of local saints, and in the method of conducting the worship of the Church. In course of time it became a source of serious practical evil which needed correction. "The abuses," writes Kellner, "resulting from the excessive multiplication of holy days [which reduced the number of working days for the poor, and encouraged others in laziness and pleasure-seeking] was remarked on

[1] See *Preface to the English Book of Common Prayer*.
[2] F. E. Warren in *Art. Liturgy in Ency. Brit.*
[3] *Articles of Religion*, XXIV.

VARIATIONS OF NATIONAL CALENDARS

by John Gerson," the great chancellor of the University of Paris, as early as the year 1408.[1]

In the matter of diversity in national calendars, one of the most striking features of the modern Roman Calendar is the peculiar emphasis which, in the course of the centuries, it has given to the festivals in honor of the mother of our Lord. While the present English Calendar has only two feast days of the first rank in her honor, namely, the Annunciation on March 25th (concerning which even Kellner says that it was "formerly regarded more as a festival of our Lord than of our Lady");[2] and the Purification on February 2d; and one black-letter day, the Nativity of the Virgin Mary, on September 8th; the Roman Calendar has five others, none of them of early origin. These are as follows:

1. **The Death and Assumption** (that is, her bodily taking-up into heaven), on August 15th, was instituted in the seventh century to celebrate her death only. The *Assumption* was a later addition, founded on a mere local legend. Kellner says, "Among the Latins the festival did not at first bear the name of *Assumption*, but was called *Domitio* or *Pausatio*," that is, *Sleep* or *Repose*.[3]

2. **The Immaculate Conception** on December 8th was "originally only a *festum Conceptionis B.V.M.* . . . If we consult the service-books printed before 1854," writes Kellner, "we find in them indeed on the 8th of December the *festum Conceptionis*, but the word *Immaculata* is nowhere found in the office for the feast."[4] Even when *Conception*, without *Immaculate*, was introduced into England in the twelfth century, Kellner adds, "two Bishops, Roger of Salisbury, and Bernard of S. Davids,

[1] Kellner, *Heortology*, p. 30. [2] Ib., p. 231.
[3] Ib., p. 238. [4] Ib., p. 241.

held a synod, and forbade the feast as an absurd novelty."[1] So also, "the greatest doctor of the thirteenth century, Thomas Aquinas," states that the Roman Church did not celebrate even the feast of the *Conception*, though she tolerated the practice of other Churches which did celebrate it.[2] Moreover, it was not until Dec. 8, 1854, that the word *Immaculate* was added, by an ordinance of Pope Pius IX.

3. **The Name of Mary,** celebrated on the Sunday after the **Nativity of our Lady,** was "first authorized by the Apostolic See [Rome] for the diocese of Cuença, in Spain, in 1513."[3]

4. **The Presentation of our Lady in the Temple,** November 21st, was "introduced into the West" in the fourteenth century.[4]

5. **The Visitation,** July 2d. "The earliest traces of the feast are found in the thirteenth century."[5]

To these may be added the minor festivals of S. Mary of the Snows, The Espousals, The Seven Sorrows, The Rosary, Blessed Mary of Mount Carmel, The Expectation of Delivery, and still others.[6]

The extraordinary growth of the *cultus* of the Blessed Virgin is seen in the fact that *no festival of the Virgin was celebrated in the Church of Rome before the seventh century.*[7]

The commemoration of **All Souls** on November 2d does not appear until the ninth century, and "it was not until the close of the tenth century, under the special impetus supplied by the reported vision of a pilgrim from Jerusalem, who declared that he had seen the tortures of the souls suffering purgatorial fire, that

---

[1] Kellner, p. 250.   [2] Dowden, p. 55.   [3] Kellner, p. 264.
[4] Ib., p. 266.   [5] Ib., p. 267.
[6] See the *Catholic Dictionary*.   [7] Dowden, xv.

VARIATIONS OF NATIONAL CALENDARS 129

the observance made headway."[1] The **Feast of Corpus Christi** (Body of Christ), which now ranks as one of the highest festivals in the Roman Calendar ("a double of the first class"), was not officially adopted till the fourteenth century.

The Orthodox Church of the East has thirteen festivals of the first rank, with their corresponding English names as follows: Christmas, Epiphany, the Purification, the Annunciation, Palm Sunday, Easter, the Ascension, Pentecost, the Transfiguration, August 6th; the Repose of the Blessed Virgin, or Theotokos, August 15th; the Nativity of the Blessed Virgin, or Theotokos, September 8th; the Exaltation of the Cross, September 14th; the Entrance of the Blessed Virgin, or Theotokos, into the Temple, November 21st. Next in dignity to these are four festivals of high rank: the Circumcision, January 1st; the Nativity of S. John Baptist, June 24th; S. Peter and S. Paul, June 29th; the Beheading of S. John Baptist, Aug. 29th.[2] Four other days are observed in honor of the Blessed Virgin, July 2d, August 31st, December 9th (the Conception), and December 26th (the Flight into Egypt, supposed to be one year and a day after the birth).[3]

The Russian Calendar corresponds largely to the Greek or Byzantine, but there are of course in all calendars, besides these and the Roman, many commemorations of persons and events peculiar to each Church. "The Eastern Calendars contrast in a striking way with the Western in the prominence given to commemoration of the saints and heroes of the Old Testament. All the prophets and many of the righteous men of Hebrew history have their days."[4]

[1] Dowden, xiv.
[3] Ib., p. 57.
[2] Ib., p. 135.
[4] Ib., 137.

APPENDIX

THE LITURGICAL COLORS

DIFFERENT colors in altar hangings, vestments, stoles, etc., have been in use in the Church for many centuries, in order to mark to the eye the different character of the seasons and days of the Christian Year. This custom does not seem, however, to have been employed before the ninth century. Kellner says, "For many centuries the liturgical vestments were exclusively white. The writers of the Carolingian period were the first to remember that different colors were used in the vestments of the Jewish High Priest." [1]

The following account of the use of colors in the worship of the Church is taken in substance from "The Ritual Reason Why," by Charles Walker.[2]

The usual colors employed in modern times are white, red, violet, green, and black. According to the old English use, blue, brown, gray, and yellow were also employed. *White* is used on all the great festivals of our Lord, of the Blessed Virgin, and of all Saints who did not suffer martyrdom; white being the color appropriate to joy, and signifying purity. *Red* is used on the feasts of martyrs, typifying that they shed their blood for the testimony of Jesus, and at Whitsuntide, when the Holy Ghost

[1] *Heortology*, p. 428.
[2] J. T. Hayes, London, 1868.

descended in the likeness of fire. *Violet* is the penitential color, and is used in Advent, Lent, Vigils, etc. *Green* is the ordinary color for days that are neither feasts nor fasts, as being the pervading color of nature, or as typifying the Resurrection. *Black* is made use of at funerals, and on Good Friday. (Many, however, prefer to use violet at funerals.)

In the old English use, *red* was employed on all Sundays throughout the year, except from Easter to Whitsunday, unless a festival superseded the Sunday services. The same color served for Ash Wednesday, Good Friday, Maundy Thursday, and Easter and Whitsun Eves. *White* was employed throughout Eastertide, whether a Sunday or a Saint's Day. *Yellow* was employed for the feasts of Confessors. *Blue* was used indifferently with green; and *brown* or *gray* with *violet* for penitential times.

LEADING QUESTIONS FOR REVIEW OR EXAMINATION

1. What are some of the practical purposes of the observance of the Christian Year?

2. Give some reasons for such a system being in accord with human needs.

3. State some of the objections of the Puritans, and the answers of the "Judicious" Hooker.

4. In what relation does the Church of Christ, in its ministry and sacraments, stand to the Church of Israel, as described by Isaiah?

5. Give some account of the Ritual Year of the Church of Israel.

6. In what way did the Jewish customs of fast and festival affect the Church of Christ?

7. Give some examples of our Lord's loyalty to the Church of His forefathers.

8. What is there remarkable in this connection as to the traditional date of His Birth?

9. What is there still more remarkable in the exact day of His Crucifixion, and of His sending of the Holy Ghost?

10. Besides His thus honoring these ancient sacred days, what practical reason did our Lord have in deliberately choosing them for certain events in His own life?

11. What hints do we find in the New Testament of the beginnings of a Christian Year in the days of the Apostles?

12. In view of ancient Jewish custom what was there remarkable in the adoption of Sunday, or the first day of the week, instead of Saturday, or the seventh day according to the Jewish reckoning?

13. Show that the change was nevertheless not contrary to either the spirit or the letter of the Fourth Commandment.

14. What clue have we to those unwritten instructions which, S. Luke (Acts i. 4) tells us, our Lord gave to His Apostles during the great forty days between His Resurrection and His Ascension?

15. What evident reasons did our Lord have for not writing, or commanding others to write, a record of His teaching?

16. What great value does this give to "acts" of Apostles, and to "traditions," "customs," and "ways" of the Church while the Apostles were still living?

17. What test does S. John, in his epistles, apply to such traditions, customs, and ways?

18. Give some examples of traditions and customs freely practised by modern denominations of Christians, yet without any written command for them in the New Testament.

19. What then is the purpose of the New Testament as declared by S. Luke in Acts i. 4?

---

20. When was the term *Anno Domini* (Year of our Lord) by which we date our years adopted, and why was it not adopted earlier?

21. Explain the terms "Old Style" and "New Style," and give the reason for the error in the Calendar which occasioned them.

22. Explain the words Cycle, Golden Number, Paschal Moon, Dominical Letter, Bissextile, Ferial and Festal, Vigil and Eve, Octave, Movable and Immovable Feasts.

23. Name the chief seasons of the Christian Year, and the Immovable Feasts of our Lord, in their order.

24. While the Calendars of national Churches differ in details, in what main features are they all agreed, thus testifying to a common origin?

25. In what way is Christmas the fulfilment of the ancient feast of Tabernacles?

26. If, as is probable, December 25 and June 24 are the actual days of the only two Nativities observed, both of them miraculous, what striking fitness is there in their occurrence just after the winter and the summer solstice?

27. To what must we attribute the immense importance attached universally by the early Church to the proper observance of Easter?

28. What is the Church's rule, in the Preface to the Book of Common Prayer, as to the proper day for Easter?

29. Give the historical reasons why all the Movable Feasts are dependent on the position of the moon in the heavens, while the Immovable Feasts are dependent on the sun.

QUESTIONS FOR REVIEW OR EXAMINATION

30. On what grounds, and by what great Council of the Church, were the controversies concerning the keeping of Easter always on a Sunday, instead of on any other day of the week, finally settled?

31. How did it happen that the British and Irish rule for the day on which to observe Easter differed from that of Italy, and of the Eastern Churches?

32. Why has the Church always attached so much importance to the observance of Ascension-day, and in what special ways does she do so?

33. Why did the Grecian Jews give the name of Pentecost to what the Hebrew-speaking Jews called the Feast of Weeks, and of Harvest?

34. In what ways was the first Christian Whitsunday the fulfilment of, and a contrast to, the first Jewish Pentecost? (See Keble's *Christian Year*, Whitsunday.)

35. Why is Trinity Sunday a fitting close to the great doctrinal division of the Christian Year?

---

36. Give Hooker's reasons for the observance of Saints' Days, and some account of their origin.

37. What is meant by "Red-letter" and "Black-letter" days?

38. Why is a Saint's Day called *Dies Natalis*, or Birthday?

39. Explain the appropriateness of the dates for the only two Nativities in the Calendar, and for some of the Saints' Days.

40. What prominence is given, in both the New and the Old Testament, to the ministration of Angels to men, and what great practical purpose is meant to be served by this clear revelation?

41. What important truth concerning the condition of the departed does All Saints' Day help us to bear in mind?

42. Give some of the Scripture reasons for the practice of fasting, and for the observance of fast days.

43. Explain the words Septuagesima, Sexagesima, Quinquagesima, and Quadragesima.

44. Give some account of the origin of Lent.

45. Explain the words Passion Week, Holy Week, Palm Sunday, and Maundy Thursday.

46. Explain why Good Friday was originally kept as a feast day, and how the change in its observance came about.

47. What is the evident intention of the Anglican Communion in regard to celebrating the Holy Communion on Good Friday?

48. Give some account of the other days of fasting and abstinence appointed in our Calendar.

49. What is the strict meaning of the word Liturgy, and the word Use when employed in connection with a Liturgy?

50. To what does the identity of the leading features of all ancient Liturgies, in spite of many local "uses" and revisions, distinctly testify?

INDEX

A

Ab, 19
Abib, 16, 17, 19
Adar, 19
Advent, 54
Agnes, S., 76, 93
Alban, S., 76, 92, 95
Alexander, Archbishop, 41
Alexander, Mrs., vii
Alexandria, 47, 67
Almanac, 44
All Hallows, 87
All Saints, 82, 87-90
All Souls, 128
Ambrose, S., 33, 76
American Prayer Book, 62, 76, 90, 121
American Revolution, 44
Andrew, S., 78, 79
Angels, 55, 82-86
Anglo-Saxons, 68
Anicetus, Bp., 66
Anne, S., 96
Anno Domini, 44
Annotated Prayer Book, see Blunt.
Annunciation, 62
Antioch, 79
Antiochus Epiphanes, 19
Antiquities of the Christian Church, see Bingham.
Apostles as Jews, 22-27

Apostolic Constitutions, 33
Aquinas, 128
Arezzo, 69
Arian Heresy, 59, 73
Armenian Church, 53, 56, 58
Articles of Religion, 38, 69, 126
Ascension-day, 68
Ash-Wednesday, 104, 107-109
Assumption, 127
Assyrians, 3
Athanasius, S., 76, 77
Atonement, Day of, 19, 21
A. U. C., 43
Augustine of Canterbury, 68, 76, 107
Augustine of Hippo, 7, 12, 33, 58, 69, 76, 78, 112
Augustus, Emperor, 55

B

Bacon, Lord, 5
Baptism of Infants, 39
B. C., 43
Becket, 72
Bede, Venerable, 69, 76, 92, 95
Benedict, S., 94
"Beginning, From the," 38, 40
"Bible only," 40
Bingham, vi, 112
Bissextile, 50
Black-letter days, 76, 92-100

INDEX

Blunt, J. H., 96, 100, 108, 109, 112, 117
Boniface, S., 76, 95
British Church, see English Church.
Brooks, Phillips, 104
Butler, Archer, 1
Byzantine Calendar, 129

C

Cæsar, Julius, 45
Calendar, 43–46, 93–100, 124–129. See also Seabury.
Calends, 45
Candlemas, 55, 61
Canon of New Testament, 39
Canterbury, 125
Carême, 106
Carthage, 39, 112
Caswall, E., vii
Ceremonies, Value of, 35
Charles I., 99
Chisleu, 19
Christ a loyal Jew, 22–27
Christian Ballads, see Coxe.
Christian Year in New Testament, 11, 12
Christmas, 8, 9, 46, 54–56, 78
Chrysostom, S., 37, 55, 70
Church, Dean, 117
"Church, The," 30, 31
Circumcision, 58, 59
Civil festivals, 3
Clemens of Alexandria, 55
Colors, Liturgical, 131, 132
Columba, S., 36, 76
Communion, Holy, 32, 39, 55, 111–113, 116, 117
Conception, Feast of, 127, 128
Confirmation, 39
Confessors, 93–98, 132
Constantine, Emperor, 34

Conversion of S. Paul, 78
Coptic Church, 53
Corpus Christi, 129
Coxe, Bp., vi, 4, 43, 47, 53, 58, 92, 110, 113, 118, 121
Creed, Nicene, 39
Crispin, S., 98
Cross-quarter, 96, 98
Customs, 35–40
Cycle, 47, 67
Cyprian, S., 76, 77, 97

D

David, S., 76, 93
Dedication, Feast of, 18–20, 24
Denys, S., 97
Dies Domini, 49
Dies Mandati, 112
Dies Natalis, 78
Dionysius Exiguus, 44
Dominical Letters, 49
Domitio of B. V., 127
Dowden, Bp., v, 33, 51, 72, 100, 112, 115, 116, 128, 129
Duchesne, vi, 55–57, 62, 107, 110

E

Easter, 29, 32, 61, 64, 65–68
Easter Even, 117–119
Eastern Church, 72, 129
Ecclesiastical Polity, see Hooker.
Edersheim, 17, 20
Egypt, 3, 67
Ellicott, Bp., 80
Elul, 19
Ember Days, 120, 121
English Calendar, 93–100
English Church, 7, 62, 68, 76, 92, 107, 125, 126
English Parliament, 8, 46, 62
Epact, 48

INDEX

Epiphany, 46, 60, 61, 67
Esther, 19, 20
Eucharist, see Communion, Holy.
Eusebius, 34, 66
Eutychus, 34
Eves, 51, 123

F
Fasting, 101–105, 120–123
Fasts, Jewish, 19
Ferial and Festal, 50, 51
"First day of the week," 32
First Fruits, 71
"Form of sound words," 39
Fortunatus, 64, 110
Fourth Commandment, 32
French Church, see Gallican.
French Revolution, 3, 44
Fridays, 122
Froude, R. H., 101

G
Gabriel, 83
Gallican Church, 69, 125
Gelasius, 125
Gentile Christians, 32, 61
George, S., 94
German Church, 73, 95
Gerson, 127
Gervase, 72
Golden Number, 48
Good Friday, 64, 104, 114–119
Greek Calendar, 129
Greek Church, 46
Greeks, 3, 43
Gregorian Calendar, 47
Gregory, Dean, 117
Gregory Nazianzen, 70
Gregory I, or the Great, 68, 76, 94, 107, 125
Gwyn, 72
Gwynne, W., see Paradise.

H
Hallowe'en, 87
Haman, 18
Harvest, Feast of, 18, 71
Hawkins, Dr. E., 41
Helena, Empress, 69
Heortology, see Kellner.
Herbert, George, 101, 103, 106, 122
Hilary, 76, 93
Hippolytus, 55
Holland, Scott, 41
Holy Communion, see Communion.
Holy Cross Day, 97
Holy Thursday, 69
Holy Week, 110–119
Hook, Dean, 41
Hooker, v, 5–8, 75, 86
How, Bp. W. W., 75, 90
Hugh, S., 76, 98
Huntington, Bp. F. D., 8
Hypapante, 61

I
Ignatius, S., 39, 76, 79
Immaculate Conception, 127
Immovable Feasts, 52, 58
Ingathering, Feast of, 18
Invention of the Cross, 94
Irenæus, 66, 107
Irish Church, 36, 51, 68, 73, 76, 121, 123–126
Isaiah, 13
Israel, Church of, 11–21
Iyyar, 19

J
James, Liturgy of S., 87, 124
Jerome, S., 76, 97
JESUS, Name of, 59, 60

INDEX

Jewish Cycle, 48, 67
Jewish Hours of the Day, 34
John Baptist, S., 78, 95
John the Evangelist, 38, 94
John XXII, 72
Johnson, J., 116
Julius I., 55

K

Keble, J., vii, 59, 61, 62, 70, 87, 114, 118
Kellner, v, vii, 1, 55, 127, 128, 131
Ken, Bp., vii
Kersmis, 55
King, Bp., 117
Kingdom of God, and Heaven, 30, 31

L

Ladyday, 62, 127
Lammas, 55, 96
Leap Year, 49, 50
Lent, 101, 104, 106-119
Leo I, 125
Liddon, Dr. H. P., 7
Lights, Feast of, 18, 19
Littledale, Dr. R. F., 124
"Liturgical Proper," 92
Liturgies, 124-126
Lord's Day, 32, 33
Lunar Cycle, 47, 48
Lyons, 79
Lyra Apostolica, vii

M

Maccabees, 17, 19, 20, 24
Maclagan, Bp., 100
Malo, or Machutus, S., 98
Mamertus, Bp., 121
Marchesvan, 19
Martene, 116

Martinmas, 98
Martyr, Justin, 17
Mary, Virgin, 127-129
Mass, 55
Maundy Thursday, 111-113
Meton, 47, 48
Metonic Cycle, 47, 48, 67
Mi-Carême, 109
Michaelmas, 55, 82-86
Mid-Lent Sunday, 109
Milan, 33
Ministry of Grace, see J. Wordsworth.
Ministry, Holy, 38, 39
Missal, 125
Monica, 33
Months, 45
Moon, New and Full, 9, 18, 47, 67
Movable Feasts, 52, 64-74

N

Nadolig, 55
Name of JESUS, 59, 60
Natale, 55
Natalis Calicis, 112
Natalis Invicti, 57
Nativity, of S. John Baptist, 78
Nativity, The, 55
Neale, Dr. J. M., 124
Newman, Dr. J. H., 76, 77, 80, 82
New Moon, 18, 67
New Style, 46
New Year, 18, 21
Nice, or Nicæa, Council of, 39, 48, 67, 107, 116
Nisan, 16, 19
Noel, 55
Norman Conquest, 44, 125
Notitia Eucharistica, see Scudamore.

INDEX

O

Octave, 51, 72
"Old Style," 46
Olympiads, 43
Ordinal, 39
Oriental Churches, 46
Origen, 70
Origines du Culte Chrétien, see Duchesne.
Orthodox Church, 46, 129
Osmund, Bp., 125
Ostera, 65

P

Palgrave, vii
Palm Sunday, 108, 110
Papists' Conspiracy, 99
Pâques, 65
Paradise, 88–90
Parliament, English, 8, 46, 62
Pascha, 29, 65, 115
Paschal Lamb, 64
Paschal Moon, see Moon.
Passion Sunday, 110
Passover, 16, 20, 24, 29, 64, 115
Patrick, S., 68
Paul, Cathedral of S., 117, 126
Paul, Conversion of S., 78, 93
Pausatio, 127
Pentecost, 17, 25, 28, 29, 71
Perpetua, S., 76
Persecutions, 33
Pesach, 16, 65
Pfingstentag, 71
Picts, 36
Pius IX., 128
Poetry of the Christian Year, vii
Polycarp, 76, 79
Polycrates, 66
Prayer Book Commentary, 55

Pre-Lent, 106, 107
Presentation of Christ, 61
Primes, 48
Primitive Liturgies, 124
Pro-anaphora, 124
"Protestants, Religion of," 40
Purification, Feast of, 55, 61
Purim, 18, 20
Puritans, 7–9

Q

Quadragesima, 106, 107
Quaresme, 106
Quartodeciman, 65, 68
Quatember, 120
Quatre Temps, Quatuor Tempora, 120

R

Raphael, 83
Red-letter Days, 76, 77
Refreshment Sunday, 109
Religio Illicita, 33
Revision of Calendars, 124–126
Ritual Year, 1–6, 40
Rogation Days, 121
Roman Calendar, 127, 128
Roman Liturgy, 125
Romans, 3, 33
Russian Church, 46, 129

S

Sabaoth, 83
Sabbath, 9, 10, 15, 16
Saints' Days, 75–90
Salisbury, and Sarum, 62, 92, 125
Sapientia, O, 99
Saravia, Dr., 86
Saturnalia, 56
Scottish Church, 36, 54, 68, 125, 126

Scripture, Holy, 39, 40, 41
Scudamore, 37, 116
Seabury, vi, 8, 45, 47-49, 67
Septuagesima, 107
Seventh Day Baptists, 31
Sexagesima, 107
Shakespeare, 5, 98, 109
Shebat, 19
Shipley, Orby, vii
Shrove Tuesday, 109
Silvia, Pilgrimage of, 69, 110
Sinai, 26, 29
Sivan, 19
Skeat, Prof., 120
Smyrna, 79
Socrates, 107
Some Purposes of Paradise, 83, 88, 89, 90
Sosigenes, 45
South, Dr., 8
Sozomen, 34, 107
Spenser, Edmund, 85, 86
Staley, v
Stanley, Dean, 63
Stedman, E. C., 120
Stephen, S., 79, 99
"Still Week," 110
Sulgwyn, 72
Sunday, 30, 31
Sunday Letter, 49
Sundays after Epiphany, 61
Sursum Corda, 37, 124
Swithin, S., 95, 96
Synagogue, 39

T

Tabernacles, Feast of, 18, 56
Tammuz, 19
Tebeth, 19
Temple, Destruction of, 19, 24
Temple, Worship of, 22, 39
Tennyson, vii, 85

Ter-Sanctus, 124
Tertullian, 17, 107
Thanksgiving Day, 90, 91
Theophany, 60
Theory and Use of the Church Calendar, see Seabury.
Theotokos, 129
Thomas, S., 78, 99
Thoughts on the Services, see Coxe.
Three Kings, Feast of the, 60, 61
Thursday, Holy, 69, 113
Tishri, 17, 19
Tobit, 17, 83
Torch-race, 37
Traditions, 35-42
Transfiguration, 58, 62, 63, 96
Translation (Reinterment), 95-98
Trinity Sunday, 72
Troas, 32, 34
Trumpets, Feast of, 18, 21

U

Unleavened Bread, Feast of, 17
Uriel, 83
"Uses," 125

V

Vernal Equinox, 67
Vestments, 40
Victor, Bp., 66
Vienne, 79
Vigil, 51, 123
Virgin Mary, see Mary.

W

Walker, Charles, 131
Walton, Isaac, 86
"Way, The," 35
Ways, 35-40

Weeks, Feast of, 18, 71
Weinachsfest, 55
Welsh Church, 68, 72
Westcott, Bp., 79
Whitsunday, 70–72
Williams, Isaac, vii

Wordsworth, Bp. John, vi, 78, 100
Wordsworth, William, vii, 1, 105

Y

Yule, 55